Northwest Happenings Guide

2015 Washington Edition
By: Catherine Pittman

Your Guide to Bazaars, Fairs, Festivals, Parades,
Carnivals, Craft Shows, Farmers Markets Fireworks and
Other Oregon Events & Attractions
From July 2015 – June 2016

A Product of the Northwest Happenings Guide
A Subsidiary of Pitter Patter Productions
Tualatin, Oregon

Distributed by

The Northwest Happenings Guide
A Subsidiary of Pitter Patter Productions

Visit Us Online!

www.pitterpatterproductions.com
www.NWhappeningsguide.com

Dedication

To Seeking Fun in Our Own Backyard,
Letting Our Inner Child Free,
Discovering Our Artistic Muse
And Living Life to Its Fullest!

Cover Design By:

Catherine Pittman

Cover Images Used With Permission

Top Left: Oktoberfest © Oaks Park Association

Top Center: Oregon Coast Historical Railway
Christmas Lights, Coos Bay, OR
© Victoria Ditkovsky
Dreamstime.com ID 47720446

Top Right: Multnomah Falls © Brigitte Werner
All Free Downloads

Center Right: Pioneer Log Fortress Defense Tower
Ft. Vancouver, WA © Capricornis
Dreamstime.com ID 7546563

Center Image: Oregon State Shape Mount Hood
Design by: Catherine Pittman
Mount Hood Image by: TPSDave
All Free Downloads

Center Left: Harney County Royalty
© Harney County Fair Association

Lower Left: Seattle Skyline Fireworks – Alki Park
© Nilanjan Bhattacharya
Dreamstime.com ID 10915928

Lower Left 2: Mountain Biking © Jacek Chabraszewski
Dreamstime.com IE 33792755

Lower Center Left Group:

   Top Left: Playful Sea Otter © Peng Ge
Dreamstime.com ID 42259797

   Top Right: Festa Italiana
© Festa Italiana Association

   Lower Left: Oregon Coast © Bill Kuffrey
All Free Downloads

   Lower Right: Whale Watching Image © Jorge Felix
Dreamstime.com ID 4275261

Lower Right
Corner: Happy Boy Riding Horse
© Crazy80frog
Dreamstime.com ID 26278058

The Northwest Happenings Guide

2015 Oregon or Washington Editions
July 2015 - June 2016

Who is the guide for?
- Families seeking kid-friendly events & attractions
- Artisans and Crafters seeking exhibit space
- Food vendors seeking vendor space
- Promotors seeking visitors & vendors
- Visitors to the Northwest seeking local, fun attractions

What type of events are in the guide?
- Bazaars
- Carnivals
- Fairs - County, State, Street & Neighborhood Fairs
- Festivals
- Farmers Markets
- Local Year-Round Attractions & Amusement Parks
- Baby & Kid Shows
- Bridal Shows
- Home Remodel & RV Shows
- Halloween Mazes, Pumpkin Farms & Haunted Houses
- Christmas Events
- Fireworks

How do I get my own copy?
Available in two formats: Paper and Kindle Ebook on
Amazon.com or www.nwhappeningsguide.com. Paper
version also available on CreateSpace.com

The Northwest Happenings Guide
A Subsidiary of Pitter Patter Productions
Tualatin, Oregon
www.NWhappeningsguide.com www.pitterpatterproductions.com

Craft Shows

Bazaars   Food Vendors

Arts & Crafts   Music Festivals

Holiday Fun   **Fairs**

Farmers Markets

Carnivals

Halloween Mazes & Fright Towns

Artisan Marketplaces

County Fairs   Petting Zoos

Wine & Beer Tasting

Fireworks **Festivals**

Parades

Street Festivals

Neighborhood Fairs

Began Prior to July thru 2015

3/1/2015 - 11/30/2015
Japanese Tea Gardens
1075 Lake Washington Blvd E - Seattle, WA
(206) 684-4725

Paid Admission; Children 5 & under Free
Kid Friendly Event
Hours: Hours vary depending on the season

3/1/2015 - 11/30/2015
San Juan Safaris Whale Watch & Wildlife
2 Spring St Landing 6 - Friday Harbor, WA
www.sanjuansafaris.com   (800) 450-6858

Orca whale watching 2015 season is March - November.

Paid Admission   Kid Friendly Event
Hours: See Website for Hours

4/1/2015 - 10/31/2015
The Farmers Market of Olympia
Capital Way North & Market St - Olympia, WA
www.olympiafarmersmarket.com   (360) 352-9096

Free Admission
Hours: Thursday - Sun: 10am - 3pm

Vendor Contact: info@olympiafarmersmarket.com

---

*I drifted into a soft summertime nap under the shade of a tree
one hot July day... serenaded by the strings of a cricket's song,
with the slow gurgle of the brook accompanying with its steady,
sweet beat. I hear a little frog join in the melody of summer and
I grow drowsy with warm dreams of summertimes past.*
~~Catherine Pittman © 2015

4/3/2015 - 12/19/2015
Bellingham Farmers Market - Downtown
1100 Railroad Ave - Bellingham, WA
www.bellinghamfarmers.org   (360) 647-2060

On the last Saturday of the month, we encourage kids to vend at the Market. This is the perfect opportunity for your child to learn how commerce and raising money works. Whether they sell what they grow or sell an original handmade art & craft item, they will have fun and earn just a little more than pocket change! Market hosts produce, arts & crafts, food & drink and demos.

Free Admission
Hours: Saturdays, 10am - 3pm

4/4/2015 - 10/10/2015
Coupeville Farmers Market
Whidbey Island - Coupville Community Green
Coupeville, WA
Like Us on Facebook!   (425) 280-4150

Ice cream, locally roasted organic coffee, fresh veggies & fruits, berries, arts & crafts, garden plants and more!

Free Admission
Hours: Saturdays, 10am - 2pm

Vendor Contact: Sarah Dylan Jensen
snohomishfarmersmarket@gmail.com

4/4/2015 - 10/31/2015
San Juan Island Farmers Market
Brickworks Plaza - San Juan Island, WA
www.sjifarmersmarket.com

Free Admission
Hours: Saturdays, 10am - 1pm

Vendor Contact: Anna Coffelt (378-3724) or Candace Jagel (378-4009) manager@sjifarmersmarket.com
# of Vendors: Limited Spaces

4/4/2015 - 12/19/2015
Vashon Farmers Market
17519 Vashon Hwy SW - Vashon, WA
www.vigavashon.org   (206) 778-8001 (Cell #)

Free Admission
Hours: Wed & Sat: 10am - 2pm

Vendor Contact: Market Manager
marketmanager@vigavashon.org

5/2/2015 - 10/31/2015
Downtown Farmers Market
Downtown - 4th & Main - Walla Walla, WA
www.farmersmarket.downtownwallawalla.com

Free Admission
Hours: Saturdays, 9am-1pm

5/21/2015 - 10/1/2015
Lake Chelan Evening Farmers Market
Riverwalk Park - Lake Chelan, WA
www.chelanfarmersmarket.org   (800) 424-3526

Many of the produce at this market comes from certified
organic farms. You'll find plenty of dairy and produce!

Free Admission
Hours: Thursdays 4pm - 7pm

# of Vendors: 15

5/27/2015 - 9/24/2015
Snohomish Farmers Market
Downtown - 1st Street & Cedar - Snohomish, WA
www.snohomishfarmersmarket.com

Free Admission
Hours: Thursdays, 3pm - 7:30 pm

6/3/2015 - 9/30/2015
Camas Farmers Market
Historic Downtown - Camas, WA
www.camasfarmersmarket.org

Free Admission
Hours: Wednesdays, 3pm - 7pm

Vendor Contact: Thomas Brundage
thomas@camasfarmersmarket.org

6/5/2015 - 10/2/2015
Bothell Farmers Market
Country Village Shops - Bothell, WA
http://www.countryvillagebothell.com
(425) 483-2250

Fresh cut flowers, fresh bread, eggs, organic produce, honey, james, and handmade wares from local artisans including, soaps, candles and more. Local musicians will entertain you with family-friendly music. There are also over 40 locally owned hops and restaurants as well as activities for the kids!

Free Admission   Kid Friendly Event
Hours: Every Friday, noon - 6pm

© Stux
All Free
Download

6/5/2015 - 10/30/2015
Market at the Parkway
The Parkway between Jadwin Ave & George Washington
Way - Richland, WA
www.marketattheparkway.com

Enjoy the "simple pleasures of the season!" Variety of
produce, nuts, berries, flowers, arts and crafts, wine, live
music and more!

Free Admission   Hours: Fridays, 9am-1pm

Vendor Contact: Kathy Hanson, (509) 539-7229
herbsetal@pocketinet.com

6/12/2015 - 10/9/2015
Columbia-Pacific Market
Veteran's Field - 3rd St & Oregon Ave N
Long Beach, WA   Like Us on Facebook!

Free Admission   Hours: Friday's 3-6pm

6/20/2015 - 9/6/2015
Birch Bay Waterslides
4874 Birch Bay-Lynden Rd - Exit 270 - Birch Bay, WA
www.birchbaywaterslides.net

Paid Admission   Kid Friendly Event
Hours: 10am - 6pm

6/25/2015 - 8/27/2015
Music in the Park Waterfront Series
Port Gardner Landing - Everett, WA
www.everettwa.gov/765/Festivals-Events
(425) 257-7117

Free Admission   Kid Friendly Event
Hours: Thursday Evenings 6:30 - 8:30 pm

Vendor Contact: Lisa Newland
lnewland@everettwa.gov

July 2015

7/2/2015 - 7/5/2015
Oak Harbor's Old-Fashioned 4th OH July
Windjammer Park - Oak Harbor, WA
www.oakharborchamber.com   360-675-3755

Oak Harbor's Old-Fashioned 4th OH July celebration includes a carnival (7/2-7/5/15), a grand parade, the Wonders of Whidbey Vendor Marketplace (food and arts & crafts), community entertainment, a Patriotic Pup Parade, a beer garden, and a huge fireworks show--all on July 4th at Windjammer Park in Oak Harbor. Come join us! oakharborchamber.com/360-675-3755

Free Admission   Kid Friendly Event
Hours: Saturday, 10am-8pm

Vendor Contact: River Powers
info@oakhaborchamber.com
# of Vendors: 30   Juried Event
Deadline: 6/19/15

7/3/2015 - 7/3/2015
Fremont Summer First Friday Art walk
New Saturn Building - Seattle, WA
www.fremontfirstfriday.com

You'll see everything from oil paintings to photography, illustrations, sculpture and mixed media. Event includes live music performances. Creativity in it's many forms!

Free Admission
# of Vendors: 20

7/3/2015 - 7/5/2015
Lake Union Wooden Boat Festival
The Center for Wooden Boats - Seattle, WA
www.cwb.org/events/festival/   (206) 382-2628

This old-fashioned, down-home waterfront event celebrates the maritime heritage of the Northwest. Free boat rides, pont boat sailing, live music, activities for kids, food and vendors, toy boat building and more.

Free Admission   Kid Friendly Event

Vendor Contact: festival@cwb.org
# of Vendors: 25   Deadline: 5/1/15
Attendance: 10000   # of Years Held: 39

7/3/2015 - 7/4/2015
Maritime Museum's Ole Fashioned 4th
Maritime Museum - Westport, WA

Crafts, music, food and fun!

Free Admission   Kid Friendly Event

7/3/2015 - 7/5/2015
Old Mill Days
32340 NE Rainier Ave - Port Gamble, WA
www.oldmilldays.com

Lumberjack Show, Chainsaw carving auction, main stage, fireworks, car show, beer garden, carnival and more!

Paid Admission   Kid Friendly Event

Vendor Contact: Johnathan Miller
jmiller@oldmilldays.com

7/4/2015 - 7/4/2015
4th of July Festival of America
Grand Coulee Dam Visitor's Center - Coulee Dam, WA
www.grandcouleedam.org

This annual event that is held in the park beneth the Grand Coulee Dam Visitor's Center features two festive days of food, arts & crafts, live music, followed by the laser light show. Immediately following the laser light show on the 4th, visitors are treated to a one-of-a-kind fireworks show that is launched from the top of the dam.

Free Admission   Kid Friendly Event

Vendor Contact: Peggy Nevsimal
peggy@grandcouleedam.org
# of Years Held: 23

7/4/2015 - 7/4/2015
An Old Fashioned Fourth of July
Peace Portal Drive & Blaine Harbor - Blaine, WA
www.blainechamber.com

Thousands of people come to celebrate the 4th with this fun-filled day long event that includes a pancake breakfast, parade, art & crafts street fair, live entertainment and plenty of yummy food! Evening ends with fireworks over the Semiahmoo Bay

Free Admission   Kid Friendly Event

Vendor Contact: info@blainechamber.com
# of Vendors: 80
Deadline: 4/1/15

If our country is worth dying for in time of war, let us resolve that it is truly worth living for in time of peace.
~~ Hamilton Fish, United States Secretary of State
1808 – 1893

7/4/2015 - 7/4/2015
Auburn 4th of July Festival
Les Grove Park - Auburn, WA
www.auburnwa.gov

Come celebrate our country's birthday in Auburn! The festival includes a noon bike parade, live entertainment on two stages, kid's craft tent, arts & crafts area with over 50 artists, car show, inflatable rides, rock wall, euro-bungy trampolines,8_ inflatable rides, a climbing wall, train rides, petting zoo, pny carousel, bingo, book sale, food concessions, a spray park and other fun activites for the whole family!

Free Admission   Kid Friendly Event
Hours: 11:00 am - 4:00 pm

Vendor Contact: Kristy Pachclarz
kpachclarz@auburnwa.gov
Deadline: 5/29/15

7/4/2015 - 7/4/2015
Bellevue Family 4th of July
Downtown Park - Belleve, WA
http://www.bellevuedowntown.com

Free Admission   Kid Friendly Event
Hours: Begins 2pm

# of Years Held: 24

7/4/2015 - 7/4/2015
Booming Bay Fireworks
Westport Marina - Westport, WA

Free Admission   Kid Friendly Event

7/4/2015 - 7/4/2015
Celebrate Independence Day FreedomFest
Cowan & Memorial Stadiums - Fort Lewis, WA
www.jblmmwr.com/freedomfest/

FreedomFest offers a day of food, fun, carnival rides, games and fireworks.

Free Admission   Kid Friendly Event
Hours: Hours: 11am - 11pm.

7/4/2015 - 7/4/2015
Colors of Freedom 4th of July Festival
Downtown & Legion Memorial Park - Everett, WA
www.everettwa.gov/765/Festivals-Events
(425) 257-7117

The day begins with the Colors of Freedom 4th of July Parade. Bring your lawn chair and grab a front row seat to start your 4th celebrations at the annual parade. The day continues at Legion Memorial Park where you can enjoy free kids activities, food fair, live music and conclude the day with a fireworks display!

Free Admission   Kid Friendly Event

Vendor Contact: Barbara Roberts
baroberts@everettwa.gov
Deadline: 6/12/15

My early childhood memories center around this typical American country store and life in a small American town, including 4th of July celebrations marked by fireworks and patriotic music played from a pavilion bandstand.
~~Frederick Reines, American Physicist 1918 – 1998

7/4/2015 - 7/4/2015
Edmonds July 4th Celebration
6th Ave N Between Bell St & Fire Dept Bldg
Edmonds, WA
www.edmondswa.com/events/fourth-of-july.html

Annual celebration includes children's parade,
Firefighter's waterball competition, food, live
entertainment, arts & crafts and fireworks!

Free Admission   Kid Friendly Event
Hours: Hours: 3:30 pm - 11pm

Vendor Contact: Sandra Williams
membership@edmondswa.com
Attendance: 150,000

7/4/2015 - 7/4/2015
Grand Old Fourth of July Celebration & Street Fair
Downtown Winslow - Bainbridge Island, WA
www.grandold4th.com

Includes an all-day street fair, classic car show, baseball
game music, food and entertainment, a beer garden and
family fun for all! Parade begins at 1pm. This fun-filled
day is capped off by the best fireworks around!

Free Admission   Kid Friendly Event

Vendor Contact: info@grandold4th.com
# of Vendors: 125
Deadline: 6/26/15
Attendance: 25000
# of Years Held: 48

This nation wil remain the land of the free only so long as it is
the home of the brave.
~~Elmer Davis, Reporter & Peabody Recipient 1890-1958

7/4/2015 - 7/25/2015
Ilwaco Summer Saturday Market
Port of Ilwaco - Ilwaco, WA
www.portofilwaco.co

Come taste smoked salmon chowder, juicy hamburgers, crunchy kettle corn, hot donuts, handmade sausage and other yummy baked goods. Stroll along the harbor front and watch the boats go by. Explore the historic vishing village of Ilwaco, and shop farm fresh produce, arts 7 crafts, potted plants and fresh-cut flowers.

Free Admission   Kid Friendly Event

Vendor Contact: satmkt.bruce@gmail.com

7/4/2015 - 7/5/2015
Pullman's 40th Annual 4th of July Celebration
Sunnyside Park - Pullman, WA
www.pullmanchambLenter.com
800-365-6948

Pullman's 40th Annual 4th of July Celebration in Sunnyside Park includes fireworks, family and fun! There is BBQ, live music by The Fabulous Kingpins and other artists, as well as many kids activities. The firework show is one you won't want to miss!

Free Admission

When an American says that he loves his country, he means not only that he loves the New England hills, the prairies glistening in the sun, the wide and rising plains, the great mountains and the sea. He means that he loves an inner air, an inner light in which freedom lives and in which a man can draw the breath of self-respect.
~~ Adlai Stevenson II, American Statesman 1900 – 1965

7/4/2015 - 7/4/2015
Ridgefield Fourth of July Festival
Downtown - Ridgefield, WA
www.ridgefield4th.com

There is something for the entire family to enjoy! Free outdoor entertainment, fun run, contests and games, foods and beverages, arts and crafts, street dance and a fabulous parade!

Free Admission   Kid Friendly Event
Hours: 10am - 6pm; fireworks at 9pm

Vendor Contact: Jodi Hunzeker - (360) 721-9164
Deadline: 6/22/15

7/4/2015 - 7/25/2015
Saturday Summer Farmers Market
Pickering Barn - Issaquah, WA
www.ci.issaquah.wa.us

Activities for kids, cooking demonstrations, farm-fresh seasonal fruits & veggies, fresh-cut flowers, freshly-baked goods, and handmade arts & crafts.

Free Admission   Kid Friendly Event

Vendor Contact: Jera Gilmore & Cynthia Wright
issaquahfarmersmarket@issaquahwa.gov
# of Vendors: 130   Juried Event
Attendance: 95000   # of Years Held: 24

7/4/2015 - 7/4/2015
Seafair Summer Fourth
Gas Works Park & Lake Union Park - Seattle, WA
www.seafair.com

Free Admission (Paid Admission for Reserved Seating)
Kid Friendly Event
Hours: Noon - 11pm

7/4/2015 - 7/4/2015
Selah 4th of July Celebration
King's Row - Selah, WA
www.easternwashingtonadventures.com

Free Admission   Kid Friendly Event

Vendor Contact: Clay Graham
selahadventures@outlook.com

7/4/2015 - 7/4/2015
Splash 2015 Annual Waterfront Festival
Chehalis River Waterfront - Aberdeen, WA
www.splash.aberdeenwa.gov

Come celebrate America's Independence in Aberdeen!

Free Admission   Kid Friendly Event
Hours: 12pm -6pm; Fireworks at 10 pm

7/4/2015 - 7/4/2015
Tacoma Freedom Fair
Ruston Way - Tacoma, WA
www.fredomfair.com

Features activities, airshows, art & craft vendors, other
exhibits, rides and fireworks!

Free Admission   Kid Friendly Event

Vendor Contact: Gary Grape gary@freedomfair.com
# of Vendors: 120
Juried Event
Attendance: 125000

7/7/2015 - 9/10/2015
Bellevue Live at Lunch
Various Venues - Bellevue, WA
www.bellevuedowntown.org

Bellevue presents the downtown Bellevue outdoor concert series, entertaining audiences with top-notch Northwest bands every Tuesday, Wednesday and Thursday at noon!

Admission: Not Provided
Attendance: 6000
# of Years Held: 24

7/9/2015 - 7/11/2015
Arlington Fly in WWII Bomber
4700 188th St NE Ste G - Arlington, WA
www.arlingtonflyin.org

Reserve your seat on the historic "Grumpy," a beautifully restored vintage North American B-25D Mitchel.

Paid Admission
Kid Friendly Event

Vendor Contact: info@arlingtonflyin.org

7/9/2015 - 8/20/2015
Children's Music in the Park Series
Thornton A Sullivan Park - Everett, WA
www.everettwa.gov/765/Festivals-Events
(425) 257-7117

Free Admission   Kid Friendly Event
Hours: Thursday Mornings 10am-11am

Vendor Contact: Lisa Newland
lnewland@everettwa.gov

7/9/2015 - 7/12/2015
Kent Cornucopia Days
Kent Commons - Kent, WA
www.kcdays.com   (253) 852-LION

This event is nationally recognized as a community service project of the Kent Lions. This premier event benefits over 250 charitable organzations. Event hosts a lot of fun: Dragon Boat Races, street fair, carnival, races, food and much more!

Admission: Not Provided
Kid Friendly Event

Vendor Contact: kentlions@gmail.com

7/10/2015 - 7/12/2015
2015 Seattle International Gem & Jewelry Show
Seattle Center – Seattle, WA
www.intergem.com

Featuring fine jewelry, gems, beads, crystals, minerals and more at the lowest possible prices. Exhibitors from all over the world will be available. Jewelry repair while you wait!

Admission: Not Provided
No Kid's Activities

Vendor Contact: info@intergem.net

...And I'm proud to be an American,
Where at least I know I'm Free.
And I won't forget the men who died,
Who gve that right to me.
~~Lee Greenwood, Musician & Songwriter

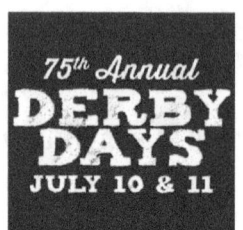

7/10/2015 - 7/11/2015
75th Annual Derby Days
157670 NE 85th St - Redmond, WA
www.redmondderbydays.com
(425) 556-2300

Redmond Derby Days is a summer festival, rooted in the spirit of competition; that celebrates the uniqueness of Redmond through parades, races, contests, game booths, carnival rides, arts, music, food and much more!

It all started in 1940 as a bike derby and parade for the community to raise money for holiday decorations and athletic equipment. Today, Derby Days celebrates Redmond's diverse community and offers all ages a chance to participate in a fun summer festival setting. Happy 75th Birthday Derby Days!

Free Admission
Kid Friendly Event
Hours: 4pm – 10pm

Vendor Contact: Rachel Van Winkle
rvanwinkle@redmond.gov
Deadline: Closed (Full)
# of Vendors: 70   Not a Juried Event
# of Years Held: 75

7/10/2015 - 7/12/2015
Chewelah Chataqua
Chewelah City Park - Chewelah, WA
www.chewelahchataqua.com

This fun-filled event has activities that wil please every member of the family: both young and young at heart! Come enjoy everything from carnival rides to a parade, food and merriment, live stage entertainment, sports, arts & crafts and more!

Admission: Not Provided
Kid Friendly Event

Vendor Contact: info@chewelahchataqua.com
Attendance: 60,000
# of Years Held: 42

7/10/2015 - 7/19/2015
Friendship With Thomas
NW Railway Museum - 38625 SE King St
Snoqualmie, WA
www.thomas.trainmuseum.org

Admission: Not Provided
Kid Friendly Event

7/10/2015 - 7/12/2015
McCleary Bear Festival
Downtown - McCleary, WA
www.mcclearybearfestival.org   (360) 495-3667

This small town festival includes kiddie parade, grand parade, bands, dances, softball tournament and many other events.

Admission: Not Provided
Kid Friendly Event

Vendor Contact: Valerie Piper bearfestival@gmail.com
Deadline: 6/19/15   # of Years Held: 56

7/10/2015 - 7/11/2015
Rhubarb Days
Heritage Park - Sumner, WA
www.rubarbtimes.com   (253) 720-9846

Lot's of fun planned: Rhubarb games, bake-off, pie
eating contest, photo contest, music, dancing and more

Admission: Not Provided
Kid Friendly Event
Hours: Sat: 10am-6pm;
             Sun: 10am-3pm

7/10/2015 - 7/12/2015
Sultan Summer Shindig Festival
River Park - Sultan, WA
www.skyvalleychamber.com/events-and-
attractions/2015-sultan-shindig/

For great small-town charm with world-class fun, come
visit the 2015 Sultan Shindig! Includes a carnival, food,
arts & crafts and live entertainment.   Carnival gates
open on Friday evening and run thru Sunday.

Admission: Not Provided
Kid Friendly Event

Vendor Contact: Debbie Copple
debbie@skyvalleyvic.net
# of Vendors: 117
Deadline: 6/15/15

Attendance: 21,000
# of Years Held: 31

---

*...To lie sometimes on the grass under the trees on a summer's
day, listening to the murmur of water, or watching the clouds
float across the blue sky, is by no means waste of time.*
~~John Lubbock, "Recreation," The Use of Life, 1894

7/10/2015 - 7/12/2015
West Seattle Summer Fest
West Seattle Junction - Seattle, WA
www.wsjunction.org/summerfest/

Come celebrate West Seattle Summer Fest... the neighborhood's largest street party of the year! The event is filled with entertainment, shopping and fun for kids of all ages. Featuring arts & crafts, beer garden, kids play area, food, live music and more!

Free Admission
Kid Friendly Event

Vendor Contact:
vendors@monumentalundertaking.com
Deadline: 4/15/15

Attendance: 35000
# of Years Held: 33

7/10/2015 - 7/12/2015
Windrider's Kite Festival
Grayland Beach - Grayland, WA
(800) 473-6018

Kite flying competition, demonstrations and games! This international event draws hundreds of participants!

Free Admission
Kid Friendly Event

I question not if thrushes sing,
If roses load the air;
Beyond my heart I need not Reach,
When all is summer there.
~~John Vance Cheney, American Poet 1848 – 1922

7/10/2015 - 7/12/2015
Yakima Folklife Festival
Yakima Valley Museum & Franklin Park: 2101 Tieton Dr
Yakima, WA
www.yakimafolklife.com/festival.html

This annual festival includes arts & crafts vendors, food fendors, music and dance performances and more. Highlight of the performances includes the Yakama Nation Dance Troupe.

Admission: Not Provided   Kid Friendly Event

Vendor Contact: info@yakimafolklife.org
Juried Event

7/11/2015 - 7/11/2015
Archaeology Kids Digs!
Ft Vancouver National Historic Site - Vancouver, WA
www.nps.gov/fova   (360) 696-7655

Kids are introduced to the world of archaeology, which includes excavation techniques, record keeping and analysis by participating in a "dig." Groups of kids will be assigned to a unit and given a box filled with soil and layers of artifacts to for their dig. As they excavate and screen with help from staff and volunteers, they will speculate about the past.

Paid Admission   Kid Friendly Event
Hours: 11am - 2pm

7/11/2015 - 7/11/2015
Art 2 Jazz Street Fair
H Street Plaza - Blaine, WA

Admission: Not Provided
Hours: 10am - 5pm

Vendor Contact: Carroll Solomon   Juried Event
Attendance: 500   # of Years Held: 25

7/11/2015 - 7/12/2015
Art By The Bay
Stanwood-Camano Fairgrounds - Stanwood, WA
www.stanwoodcamanoarts.com   (360) 770-5223

23rd annual Fine Art and Craft Festival. Great food, music and lots of parking.

Free Admission   Kid Friendly Event
Hours: Sat. - Sun 10 am. - 5 pm.

Vendor Contact: Mary Ann Hinshaw
hinshaw.guild@yahoo.com
# of Vendors: 100
Juried Event
Deadline: When Full

Attendance: 4000
# of Years Held: 23

7/11/2015 - 7/12/2015
Choochokam Arts & Music Festival
Center of Town - Langley, WA
www.choochokamarts.org   (360) 221-6765

A FREE festival with fun for the entire family! Come join us for food, art, indie music and more.

Free Admission   Kid Friendly Event
Hours: Sat: 9am-6pm;
            Sat street dance: 7pm-9:30 pm;
            Sun: 10am-5pm

Vendor Contact: info@choochokamarts.org
# of Vendors: 115
Juried Event
# of Years Held: 40

Music is what life sounds like.~~Eric Olson, Author

7/11/2015 - 7/12/2015
DragonFest & Night Market
International District - Seattle, WA
www.mobilefoodrodeo.com

Join us for the largest Pan-Asian American street fair in the Pacific Northwest! DragonFest has been a community event since 1975. Featuring an outdoor international market, dance party for all ages, shopping and entertainment, with Chinatown's largest night market in Seattle. Includes a Japanese Beer Garden, great entertainment, cultural performances and much, much more!

Admission: Not Provided
Kid Friendly Event
Hours: Saturday: 12pm - Midnight;
        Sunday: 12pm - 6pm

Vendor Contact: vendors@piranhablonde.com
# of Vendors: 100

7/11/2015 - 7/19/2015
Kla Ha Ya Days
Downtown - Snohomish, WA
www.klahayadays.com

Festival takes place through out the historic community of Snohomish. Featuring a carnival, parade, "frogtastic kids fair," live music, games, beer garden, food, wine tastings, custom classic car show, river run, arts and crafts, barbeque and more!

Admission: Not Provided
Kid Friendly Event

Vendor Contact: info@klahayadays.com

7/11/2015 - 7/11/2015
Lakewood Summerfest
Fort Stellacoom Park - Lakewood, WA
(253) 983-7887

Fun for all ages! Featuring kids activities, live
entertainment, public market, car show, Sprint Triathlon,
movie at dusk and much more!

Free Admission
Kid Friendly Event

Vendor Contact: arichardson@cityoflakewood.us
Deadline: 6/12/15

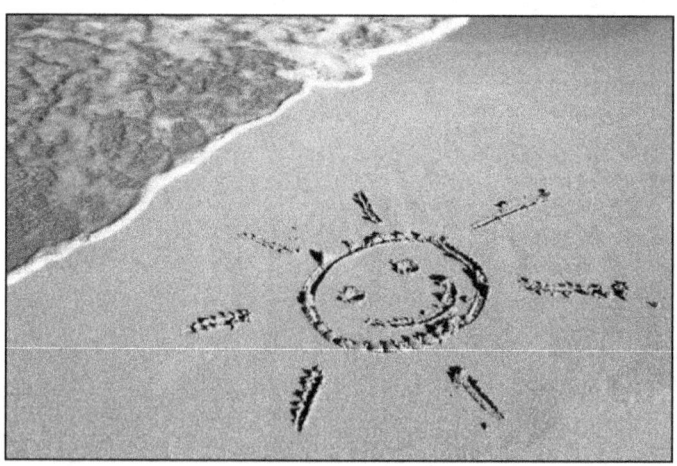

Sun in the Sand © Petr Kratochvil
All Free Downloads

7/11/2015 - 7/12/2015
Mercer Island Summer Celebration
Streets Around Mercerdale Park - Mercer Island, WA
www.misummercelebration.com   (206) 275-7864

This festival offers a variety of activities including a parade, car show, fireworks, children's fun zone, food vendors, boat rides around the island, arts & crafts booths and more. This year's event is the "Return of the Pirates!" Will have a pirate them and activites, including black powder shows, sword fighting and pirate games!

Admission: Not Provided
Kid Friendly Event

Vendor Contact: Amber Britton
amber.britton@mercergov.org
# of Vendors: 100   Juried Event
Attendance: 10000 - 20000   # of Years Held: 25

7/11/2015 - 7/12/2015
Mill Creek Festival
Mill Creek Blvd & 161st St - Mill Creek, WA
www.millcreekfestival.com   (425) 422-4721

Featuring artisan booths that feature handcrafted items only, neighborhood business booths, car show, yummy food, live entertainment, beer & wine garden, mmunity stage with local acts, children's activities and a pet plaza.

Admission: Not Provided
Kid Friendly Event
Hours: Sat: 11am-7pm;
        Sun: 11am-5pm

Vendor Contact: Linda Martin
meetmeinmillcreek.artist@yahoo.com
# of Vendors: 110

Attendance: 20000
# of Years Held: 14

7/11/2015 - 7/11/2015
Ocean Shores Beach Blast
Ocean Shores Convention Center - Ocean Shores, WA
www.oceanshoresbeachblast.com

Ocean Shores Beach is Washington's top beach destination! Featuring non-stop music, vendors, s'mores and you!

Admission: Not Provided
Kid Friendly Event

Vendor Contact: Dennis Irby
youreventpromoters@gmail.com

Attendance: 2,000

7/11/2015 - 7/12/2015
Pend Oreille Valley Lavender Festival
Woodland Park - Newport, WA
www.poviavenderfestival.com   (509) 671-0295

This garden-party atmosphere in a wooded park setting! Browse the many booths of unique artisans and growers and find that special item to take home with you! Enjoy having lunch and just sit, relax and listen to the music in the wine garden! Children's activities include making arts & crafts, games, and a marionette puppet show.

Admission: Not Provided
Kid Friendly Event
Hours: Saturday 9-5;
          Sunday 10-4

Vendor Contact: Loyce Akers
lavenderfestival@live.com
# of Vendors: 100

# of Years Held: 12

7/11/2015 - 7/12/2015
San Juan Island Summer Arts Fair
Courthouse - Friday Harbor, WA
www.sanjuanisland.org   (360) 378-5240

Largest and longest-running art extravaganza on the
islands! Filled with talented artist who show and sell
their creative works, fun local music wafting over the
courthouse lawn, food vendors, and fun for everyone!

Admission: Not Provided
Kid Friendly Event

Vendor Contact: chamber@sanjuanisland.org
# of Vendors: 50   Juried Event
Deadline: 6/20/15
Attendance: 5000

7/11/2015 - 7/11/2015
Seafair Milk Carton Derby
Green Lake - Seattle, WA
www.seafairboatclub.org/MilkCartonDerby.html

Paid Admission
Kid Friendly Evnt

Vendor Contact: David Dodge
milkcartonderby@seafairboatclub.org

7/11/2015 - 7/12/2015
SeafoodFest
Ballard Neighborhood - Seafood, WA
www.seafoodfest.org

Admission: Not Provided
Kid Friendly Event
Hours: Sat: 11am - 10pm;
        Sun: 11am - 7pm

Attendance: 65,000

7/11/2015 - 7/12/2015
Washington State Health, Fitness & Beauty Expo
Washington State Fair Showplex Events Center
Puyallup, WA
www.wastatefitnessexpo.com   (253) 335-8237

Paid Admission   No Kid's Activities
Hours: Sat: 9am - 9pm;
             Sun: 9am - 6pm

Vendor Contact: info@williamsproductions.com
# of Years Held: 13

7/11/2015 - 7/12/2015
Wedgwood Art Festival
Our Lady of the Lake Parish & School - Seattle, WA
www.wedgwoodfestival.com   (206) 523-4792

The largest neighborhood art festival in Seattle!
Featuring fine art, live bands, food trucks, kid's crafts
and more.

Admission: Not Provided   Kid Friendly Event
Hours: 10am - 5pm

Vendor Contact: Nancy Reed & Alex Strazzanti
wafestival@gmail.com
# of Vendors: 75   Juried Event
Deadline: 4/2/15

Attendance: 30,00
# of Years Held: 10

---

*Festivals are fun for kids, fun for parents and offer a welcome
break from the stresses of the nuclear family.*

*The sheer quantities of people make life easier: Loads of adults
for the adults to talk to, and loads of kids for the kids to play
with.*
~~ Tom Hodgkinson, Author

7/15/2015 - 7/19/2015
Capital Lake Fair
Heritage Park - Olympia, WA
www.lakefair.org   (360) 943-7344

Celebrating our community since 1957! Includes arts & crafts, battle of the bands car show, summer sidewalk sale, live entertainment, fireworks, food concessions, funtastic carnival, grand parade, and kids' day!

Admission: Not Provided   Kid Friendly
Event

Vendor Contact: office@lakefair.org
Juried Event

7/15/2015 - 7/19/2015
Sandsations Sand Castle Competition
Long Beach Boardwalk - Long Beach, WA
www.funbeach.com   (800) 451-2542

Cash prizes at this sand castle building contest with categories for novices and masters!   Excellent family fun!

Free Admission

7/16/2015 - 7/16/2015
Cherry Picker's Trot
10321 E Day St Spokane Rd - Mead, WA
www.greenbluffgrowers.com/events/index.html

Contestants compete in the largest "pit spitting event this side of the Rockies! Even the little folks will have fun in the free Tot Trot. Includes live music, hamburger & Hotdoogs, cherry pies and other delicious goodies.

Admission: Not Provided   Kid Friendly Event
Hours: Begins 5pm
Vendor Contact: gbdma2010@gmail.com

7/16/2015 - 7/19/2015
King County Fair
Enumclaw Expo Center - Enumclaw, WA
www.enumclawexpocenter.com   (901) 867-7007

Racing pigs, mutton bustin' midway rides, magic show, live music, kids activities, arts & crafts, food, hot tubs, playgrounds, livestock shows & exhibits and much more!

Admission: Not Provided
Kid Friendly Event

Vendor Contact: info@universalfairs.com

7/17/2015 - 7/18/2015
Algona Days
Matchett Park - Algona, WA
www.algonawa.gov/general/page/community-events   (253) 833-2897

This community event is filled with art & craft booths, food vendors, parade, and live entertainment.

Paid Admission   Kid Friendly Event
Hours: Fri: 5pm - 9pm; Sat: 10am - 6pm
Vendor Deadline: 7/10/15

7/17/2015 - 7/19/2015
Davenport Pioneer Days
Downtown - Davenport, WA
www.pioneerdays.org   (509) 263-6326

This exciting celebration features the Pioneer Plod Fun Run, Road Knights Classic Car Show, parade, Lions Club Barbeque, Belly Flop Contest, Live Music, teen dance, farmers market, vendors, beer garden and many more activities!

Admission: Not Provided   Kid Friendly Event
Vendor Contact: Dawn Tysz jenbakos77@gmail.com
Deadline: 7/10/15

"The Alley" restaurant's host, Jason Wilson   The Bite Cards' host, Thierry Rautureau "The Chef in the Hat"

GROUPON

BITE *of* **seattle**

July 17th - 19th, 2015
Seattle Center
f www.biteofseattle.com t

GREAT FOOD, MUSIC + MORE!

CRAFT BEER+ WINE

7/17/2015 - 7/19/2015
Groupon Bite of Seattle
Seattle Center - Seattle, WA
www.biteofseattle.com   (425) 295-3262

The Groupon Bite of Seattle® features 50+ restaurants and vendors, local wine and craft beer and cider tasting areas, 5 outdoor entertainment stages, a free movie night, Beer Gardens featuring local craft beer and all new local spirits signature cocktails, Seattle chefs performing live demonstrations and mystery ingredient cook-offs, a Family Fun Zone, a first of its kind social media scavenger hunt that sends event goers around the festival to win prizes, and much more!

Free Admission   Kid Friendly Event
Hours: Fri & Sat 11 a.m. - 9 p.m. Sun 11 a.m. - 8 p.m.

Vendor Contact: Festivals Inc. info@festivals-inc.com
Attendance: 400,000
# of Years Held: 34

7/17/2015 - 7/18/2015
Lynden Raspberry Festival
Downtown - Lynden, WA
www.lynden.org   (360) 354-5995

Featuring a KidZone with inflatables and activity stations, two live entertainment stages, food booths, "berry Fair" art market with handmade arts & crafts, Razz & Shine Car Show, Curt Maberry Memorial 3-on-3 Basketball Tournament and the famous Raspberry Sundae.

Admission: Not Provided   Kid Friendly Event
Hours: Fri: 10am - 8pm; Sat: 8am - 6pm

Vendor Contact: events@lynden.org
# of Vendors: 30   Juried Event
Deadline: 6/11/15
Attendance: 20,000   # of Years Held: 17

7/17/2015 - 7/19/2015
Sequim Lavender Fiesta
Jardin du Soleil - Sequim, WA
www.jardindusoleil.com   (360) 582-1185

This fun and festive event includes Latin food, drink, music and traditional crafts. Also features distillation and processing demos, kids and adults crafts, petting zoo, antique car show, garden maze and many other activities!

Free Admission
Kid Friendly Event

7/17/2015 - 7/19/2015
Vashon Island Strawberry Festival
Downtown - Vashon, WA
www.vashonchamber.com   (206) 463-6217

A jam-packed weekend of uniquely old fashioned fun, food, arts and crafts, live music, family activities, parades, carnival rides, pancake breakfast, and much, much more!

Admission: Not Provided
Kid Friendly Event
Hours: Friday: 7pm - midnight;
          Saturday: 10am - midnight;
          Sunday: 10am - 6pm

Vendor Contact: discover@vashonchamber.com
# of Vendors: 224
Attendance: 35,000
# of Years Held: 106

I entreat all artisans faithfully to follow their craft and take delight in it.
~~ Jan Hus, Cezechoslovakian Philosopher 1369 – 1415

7/18/2015 - 7/18/2015
3rd Annual Car Show 4 Kids
Coastal Farm & Ranch Parking lot,
1425 Outlet Collection Drive
Auburn, WA

www.facebook.com/carshow4kids
(253) 735-8974 between 9am-9pm

3rd Annual Car Show 4 Kids This is a fundraiser car show benefiting the Pediatric Brain Tumor Foundation. 100% of the funds go towards this great charity! $20 entry fee or $15 pre-registered by 7/11. Show off your favorite, car, truck, or motorcycle. All makes and models welcome!

Door Prizes! Raffles! Music! Miss South Sound Suzy Pin Up Contest and Bake Sale. And lots of Fun!! Dash Plaques for the first 50 entered. We had around 100 cars last year and hoping to have a lot more this year! Like us at www.facebook.com/carshow4kids. Questions? Contact Ed Britz.

Paid Admission   Kid Friendly Event
Hours: 9am to 4pm. Registration: 9am - 1pm;
          Trophies Awarded: 3pm.

Vendor Contact: Ed Britz algonataz@comcast.net
Attendance: 250   # of Years Held: 3

Shell in the Sand © Tom Genovese
All Free Downloads

7/18/2015 - 7/18/2015
Bremerton Summer Brewfest
100 2nd Street - Bremerton , WA
http://www.washingtonbeer.com
(206) 795-5510

The 5th annual Bremerton Summer Brewfest is moving to the waterfront this year, just a short walk from the Seattle - Bremerton ferry! This event features 30 Washington breweries pouring more than 100 craft beers. To celebrate the Summer, our Washington brewers will be focusing on fruit infused beers.

Paid Admission
Hours: Saturday, Noon - 6:30pm

# of Vendors: 30 breweries	Not a Juried Event
Attendance: 3,000	# of Years Held: 5

7/18/2015 - 7/18/2015
Covington Days Festival
169th Place SE - Covington, WA
www.covingtonwa.gov/covingtondays
(253) 480-2402

This event provides family fun while promoting community spirit! The festival kicks off with a parade at 10am. Afterwards, join us on the festival grounds as they come alive with arts & crafts, carnival games, exhibitors, kid and family activities, live stage entertainment, inflatable toys, watermelon eating contest, and many more activities!

Paid Admission   Kid Friendly Event
Hours: 10am - 5pm

Vendor Contact: Karla Slate kslate@covingtonwa.gov
# of Vendors: 100   Attendance: 3000 - 5000
# of Years Held: 29

7/18/2015 - 7/19/2015
Gig Harbor Summer Art Festival
Historic Waterfront District - Gig Harbor, WA
www.pennisulaartleague.com/artFest.html
(253) 853-2178

Proceeds from the annual art festival provide art
scholarships for local students and PAL members.

Paid Admission   Kid Friendly Event

Vendor Contact: Emily Ghaf emily.ghaf@gmail.com
# of Vendors: 120   Juried Event
Deadline: 2/28/15   # of Years Held: 31

7/22/2015 - 7/25/2015
Cowlitz County Fair & Rodeo
Fairgrounds - Longview, WA
www.cowlitzcountyfair.com   (360) 577-3121

Featuring kids activities, art & craft vendors, food,
rodeo, livestock shows and exhibits and contests.

Paid Admission   Kid Friendly Event

7/23/2015 - 7/26/2015
Columbia Gorge Bluegrass Festival
Skamania County Fairgrounds - Stevenson, WA
www.columbiagorgebluegrass.net (509) 427-3980

This year's line-up includes the great Laurie Lewis and
the Right Hands, Jeff Scoggins and Colorado, Sierra Hull,
The Caleb Klauder Country Band, the Downtown
Mountain Boys, Jim Faddis and FarmStrong and many
more! Join us for the 2015 event in scenic Stevenson,
Washington for this unique blend of the best in
bluegrass!

Paid Admission
Vendor Contact: jackson@co.skamania.wa.us
Attendance: 5000   # of Years Held: 32

7/24/2015 - 7/26/2015
2015 Gold Dust Days
Gold Bar Elementary School Grounds - Gold Bar, WA
www.skyvalleychamber.com

Free fun for kids includes bike decorating session & parade, bouncy house, gunny sack races against local firefighters and more. Event includes a street fair, car show gold panning, live music and much, much more!

Admission: Not Provided   Kid Friendly Event

Vendor Contact: Debbie Copple
debbie@skyvalleyvic.net   Juried Event

7/24/2015 - 7/26/2015
Bellevue Arts Museum ARTSfair
Bellevue Square & Arts Museum - Bellevue, WA
www.bellevuearts.org/fair/   (425) 519-0742

Featuring a multitude of free community arts programs, including: KIDSfair, BAM Exhibitions, delicious food and beverages. Featuring juried artists from around the continent showcasing their unique, handmade crafts and fine art.

Admission: Not Provided   Kid Friendly Event
Hours: Fri & Sa
t: 9:30am - 9:30 pm;
     Sun: 9:30 am - 6pm

Vendor Contact: Meredit Anderson
meredithl@bellevuearts.org
# of Vendors: 300   Juried Event
Deadline: 1/18/15

Attendance: 330,000
# of Years Held: 68

7/24/2015 - 7/26/2015
Bellevue Festival of the Arts
10300 NE 8th St - Bellevue, WA
www.belevuefest.org   (206) 363-2048

Located just across from Lake Washington, this festival comes complete with live entertainment! Art & craft works sold by the artists with the proceeds benefiting local charities. Features 200 of the most talented artisans, musicians and craftspeople from the Northwest.

Admission: Not Provided
Kid Friendly Event
Hours: Fri-Sat: 10am - 8pm; Sun: 10am - 6pm

Vendor Contact: info@bellevuefest.org
# of Vendors: 200   Juried Event
Attendance: 75,000   # of Years Held: 31

7/24/2015 - 7/25/2015
Camas Days
Downtown - Camas, WA   (360) 834-2472

Art & craft vendors, gated wine & microbrew street, food, concerts in the park, kid's parade and main parade, ducky derby, kids activities, softball tournament and the famous bathtub races.

Free Admission
Kid Friendly Event

Vendor Contact: Brent Erickson
# of Vendors: 145   Juried Event
Attendance: 15,000

A painter paints pictures on canvas. But musicians paint their pictures on silence.
~~ Leopold Stokowski, Brittish Conductor 1882 – 1977

7/24/2015 - 8/21/2015
Cinema Under the Stars
Thornton A Sullivan Park - Everett, WA
www.everettwa.gov/765/Festivals-Events
(425) 257-7117

Bring your blankets or lawn chairs and enjoy a movie under the stars! Snacks available on a cash only basis.

Free Admission   Kid Friendly Event
Hours: Fridays. Pre movie entertainment: 7:30pm;
          movie begins at dusk

Vendor Contact: Barbara Roberts
baroberts@everettwa.gov

7/24/2015 - 7/25/2015
Enumclaw Rotary Street Fair
Downtown - Enumclaw, WA
www.enumclawstreetfair.com   (253) 973-9735

There is something for everyone at this annual street fair. Listen to music on your way to the kid play zone, savor gourmet ice cream, funnel cakes, cotton candy and peruse the many booths of handmade wares. You are sure to find something that tickles your fancy!

Admission: Not Provided   Kid Friendly Event
Hours: 10am - 7pm

Vendor Contact: Jacklyn
jacklyn@enumclawstreetfair.com
# of Vendors: 120
Deadline: 6/30/15

Attendance: 12000
# of Years Held: 8

7/24/2015 - 7/26/2015
Kitsap Arts & Crafts Festival
Village Green Park - Kingston, WA
www.kitsapartsandcrafts.com   (360) 271-8236

Student art show, food, beer garden, live music, kid's corner and handmade crafts.   Benefits college art scholarships for local students.

Paid Admission   Kid Friendly Event

Vendor Contact: Evy Holstein evyhh@comcast.net
# of Vendors: 110   Juried Event
Deadline: 7/1/115

Attendance: 1,000
# of Years Held: 56

7/24/2015 - 7/26/2015
Lake Stevens Aquafest
Downtown - Lake Stevens, WA
www.aquafest.org   (425) 397-2344

This family-friendly event is held in beautiful downtown Lake Stevens.   The three-day festival draws crowds throughout the Northwest and Canada, boasting 60 events, such as the Grand Children's & Boat Parades, proud pet show, aquaruns, classic car show, arts & crafts, delicious northwest food, fireworks and beverage garden.

Admission: Not Provided   Kid Friendly Event
Hours: Fri: 12pm - 9pm; Sat: 10am-10pm;
        Sun: 10am-5pm

Vendor Contact: Tracy Vincent
artscrafts@aquafest.org
# of Vendors: 115   Deadline: 7/6/15

Attendance: 32,000
# of Years Held: 53

7/24/2015 - 7/26/2015
Renton River Days
Liberty Park & Cedar River Park - Renton, WA
www.rentonriverdays.org   (425) 430-6528

A Multi-day family festival and celebration of community pride, bringing residents, businesses, organizations and Puget Sound tourists together! Featuring a wonderful variety of events, special features for kids, arts & crafts, rubber ducky derby, recreation, food and live stage entertainment at Liberty and Cedar River parks.

Paid Admission   Kid Friendly Event
Hours: Fri: 11am - 8pm; Sat: 10am-8pm;
            Sun: 10am-6pm

Vendor Contact: Sonja Mejlaender
smejlaender@rentonwa.gov
# of Vendors: 95   Juried Event
Deadline: 5/10/15
Attendance: 35,000   # of Years Held: 30

7/24/2015 - 7/25/2015
Richland Art in the Park
Howard Amon Park - Richland, WA
www.alliedartsrichland.org   (509) 539-2740

Art in the Park event features artists and craftspeople offering a unique array of photography, jewelry, metal art, pottery, paintings, glass, and much more! Delicious food, fantastic music and a shuttle service also available. Funds from the event support the operation of the gallery and the ability of Allied Arts Association to give scholarships to deserving art students.

Paid Admission   Kid Friendly Event
Hours: Fri: 9am-9pm; Sat: 9am-7pm

Vendor Contact: artinthepark@alliedartsrichland.org
# of Vendors: 250   Juried Event   Deadline: 6/1/15
Attendance: 35,000   # of Years Held: 65

7/25/2015 - 7/25/2015
17th Annual Aberdeen Art Walk & Rod Fest
Historical Downtown - Aberdeen, WA
(360) 500-5763

This day of fun and entertainment is perfect for art lovers and car enthusiasts! Includes arts & crafts set-up throughout Central Downtown Aberteen, entertainers, food vendors, midnight cruisers car show!

Admission: Not Provided   Kid Friendly Event
Hours: Art & Crafts: 10am - 4pm;
           Car Show: 10am - 3pm

Vendor Contact: Kathi Prieto
kathiprieto@centurylink.net
# of Vendors: 45+   Deadline: 6/1/15
# of Years Held: 17

7/25/2015 - 7/26/2015
27th Annual Ethnic Fest Celebration
Wright Park, 501 S I St - Tacoma, WA
www.EthnicFestTacoma.org   (253) 305-1000

Celebrate our local diversity and enjoy music, food, and fun at the 27th Annual Ethnic Fest Celebration July 25th and 26th at historic Wright Park in Tacoma WA. Stay for an evening movie under the stars to kick-off our Summer Bash move in the park series! This year's celebration will feature Alchemy Skateboarding, Fab 5, Michael Powers, Asia Pacific Cultural Center (APCC), and food from around the globe! To learn more visit EthnicFestTacoma.org.

Admission: Not Provided   Kid Friendly Event

7/25/2015 - 7/26/2015
Alki Art Fair
Alki Beach Park - Seattle, WA
www.alkiartfair.org
(206) 763-6553

Alki Art Fair is West Seattle's premier summer art showcase on Alki Beach celebrating the arts and music. This annual community event is much anticipated and extremely well attended, over 10,000 in attendance last year.

The Alki Art Fair features juried arts and crafts, presented and offered for sale by artists from throughout the Puget Sound area. Performances occur on three stages during the fair. Art, music, and food annually draw visitors to Alki Beach Park to enjoy the fair's family-oriented activities on Seattle's most scenic beach.

Free Admission   Kid Friendly Event
Hours: Saturday, 10AM - 9PM Sunday, 10AM - 8PM

Vendor Contact: Frances Gifford info@alkiartfair.org
# of Vendors: 100   Juried Event
Deadline: 6/20/15
Attendance: 8,000 - 10,000   # of Years Held: 18

7/25/2015 - 7/25/2015
Country Nesters Antiques in the Park Show
John Dam Plaza Park - Richland, WA
www.countrynesters.com   (509) 430-2151

This wonderful events will help you find your antique vintage treasures

Admission: Not Provided   No Kid's Activities
Hours: 9 am - 4pm

Vendor Contact: Cheryl countrynesters@aol.com
# of Vendors: 60   Attendance: 500

7/25/2015 - 7/26/2015
Ethnic Fest 2015
Wright Park - Tacoma, WA
www.metroparkstacoma.org/ethnicfest
(253) 305-1022

Featuring the many cultures and ethnic groups that make Pierce County a great place to live! Enjoy two full days of live music, dance, art, and foods from around the world at this fun event.

Admission: Not Provided   Kid Friendly Event
Hours: Noon - 7pm

Vendor Contact: ethnicfest@tacomaparks.com
# of Years Held: 25

7/25/2015 - 7/25/2015
NW SolarFest Sustainable Living Fair
Shoreline Community College
Shoreline, WA
www.shorelinesolar.org   (206) 306-9233

Longest running, locally produced sustainable living fair in the Puget Sound region with 90+ vendors and exhibits. Learn about all the different options available for transitioning to a more sustainable lifestyle. Enjoy exhibits, participate at conversation stations, enter the Urban County Fair, and have fun in the KIDZone. Activities, food, and entertainment for all. Take the family and make a day of it.

Free Admission   Kid Friendly Event
Hours: Saturday 10am -5pm

Vendor Contact: Maryn Wynne
marynwynne@shorelinesolar.org
# of Vendors: 100   Not a Juried Event
Deadline: 7/1/15
Attendance: 4500   # of Years Held: 12

7/25/2015 - 7/26/2015
Pacific Northwest Mushroom Festival
Regional Athletic Complex - Lacey, WA
www.pnwmushroomfest.org   (360) 259-6672

Fun for the whole family! Includes great food, live music, speakers, cooking demos and activities for everyone in the family!

Admission: Not Provided   Kid Friendly Event
Hours: 10am - 6pm

Vendor Deadline: 5/15/15
# of Years Held: 8

7/25/2015 - 7/25/2015
Silvana Fair
Viking Hall - Silvana, WA
www.silvanafair.com   (360) 652-0587

Our goal? Promote community spirit and help our local youth prepare for larger fairs. Youth show many types of animals. Includes categories open to adults, organized kids games, delicious food, live music, family fun, demonstrations, and vendors offering their goods and services.

Admission: Not Provided   Kid Friendly Event
Hours: 9am - 6pm

Vendor Contact: info@silvanafair.com
# of Years Held: 66

Deserted Boat Summertime on Whidbey Island
Catherine Pittman © 2013

7/29/2015 - 8/2/2015
Thurston County Fair
Lacey Fairgrounds - Lacey, WA
www.co.thurston.wa.us   (360) 786-5453

This community event celebrates education, promotes and showcases the agricultural industry and home life of Thurston County citizens of all ages! The fair hosts contests, competitions, events and exhibits ranging from arts and crafts, photography, livestock and commercial booths. Includes kids games, free musical entertainment, great food, fun carnival rides, youth market animal sale, petting farm are just many of the fair's highlights!

Admission: Not Provided
Kid Friendly Event

Vendor Contact: bodnark@co.thurston.wa.us
# of Vendors: 100
Juried Event

7/30/2015 - 8/1/2015
Creation Festival 2015
1500 S Oak St - Kennewick, WA

Paid Admission
Vendor Contact: help@creationfest.com

*Fun in the Portland
Fountain
© Malia Autio*

7/31/2015 - 8/2/2015
Magnolia Summerfest
Magnolia Playfield - Seattle, WA
www.magnoliasummerfest.org   (206) 396-8803

Festival includes annual art show, merchants' sidewalk sale, live music, local food, arts and crafts booths, pony rides, inflatable rides, clowns and magicians, and a beer garden. Last but not least: includes the Seafair Parade and Kid's Parade.

Admission: Not Provided   Kid Friendly Event
Hours: Fri: 11am-10pm; Sat: 10am - 6pm

Vendor Contact: info@magnoliachamber.org
# of Vendors: 100   Deadline: 7/10/15
Attendance: 8000   # of Years Held: 59

7/31/2015 - 8/2/2015
Mt. Baker Rhythm & Blues Festival
Deming Logshow Grounds - Bellingham, WA
www.bakerblues.com

Featuring: Jesse James and the Mob, Midlife Crisis and the Alimony Horns, Popa Chubby, The Naughty Blokes, The Wired Band, The Fat Tones, Scott Holt, Hundred Seventy Split, Foghat, Rev Deb's Gospel Hour, Nick Vigarino, Junkyard Jane, The Kirby Sewell Band, Rick Estrin and the Nightcats, Ana Popovic.

Paid Admission   No Kid's Activities

Vendor Contact: Lloyd Petersen freesprt@televar.com
Attendance: 2000

Listen baby to the music of the night.
Hear the little cricket sing with all her might!
She will play her tiny strings, a sweet lullaby she brings,
As you slumber she will play 'til morn's first light!
~~ Lyrics, A Summer Lullaby by Catherine Pittman from The
Dream Faerie Album © 2000

7/31/2015 - 8/2/2015
Stanwood Camano Community Fair
6431 Pioneer Highway - Stanwood , WA
www.stanwoodcamanofair.org   360-629-4121

Come out and see why we're called the best lil' fair in the west. We have lots of animals, food and exhibits. We have an exciting carnival to keep the kids busy and live music to enjoy as well. This years entertainers include Strutz, El Loco, Sonic Funk Orchestra, Problem Child and many others.

Paid Admission   Kid Friendly Event
Hours: Friday 9am - 9 pm
        Saturday 9 am - 9 pm
        Sunday 9 am - 6 pm

Attendance: 12,000   # of Years Held: 83

Child in the Meadow
© George Hodan

8/1/2015 - 8/1/2015
12th Annual Index Arts Festival
Downtown - Index, WA
www.indexartsfestival.org

A celebration of the arts: Music, arts & crafts, and poets. Includes outdoor painting, crafts marketplace, live music, poetry readings, food and children's art activities!

Admission: Not Provided   Kid Friendly Event

Vendor Contact: info@indexartsfestival.org

8/1/2015 - 8/2/2015
2015 Seattle Craft Fair
Warren G Magnuson Hanger 30 - Seattle, WA
www.renegadecraft.com   (773) 227-2707

Join us for a weekend of shopping this thoughtful selection of today's finest independent handmade items.

Admission: Not Provided
Hours: 11am - 6pm

Vendor Contact: duggan@renegadecraft.com
Juried Event   Deadline: 4/27/15

What is a perfect summer day?
It is seeing the bright blue summer sky,
Hearing the melodies of nature all sing in harmony,
And feeling the sweet summer sun kiss my face.
These are the joys of the perfect summer day!
~~Catherine Pittman © 2015

8/1/2015 - 8/2/2015
Coupeville Arts & Crafts Festival
Historic Waterfront - Coupeville, WA
www.coupevillefestival.com   (800) 647-7706

One of the oldest run festivals in Washington, we're celebrating our 51st year! Festival is known for its quality, handmade crafts from artisans in the Pacific Northwest and behond. 200 Booths fill this charming, historic town of Coupeville, located on Whidbey Island. You'll find children's activities, food, restaurants, wine garden and live musical entertainment. It's fun for all!

Paid Admission   Kid Friendly Event
Hours: Sat: 10am - 6pm; Sun: 10am - 5pm

Vendor Contact:
info@coupevilleartsandcraftsfestival.org
# of Vendors: 200   Juried Event
# of Years Held: 52

8/1/2015 - 8/1/2015
Cowboy Caviar Fete
Community Hall - Conconully, WA
www.conconully.com   (877) 826-9050

This ranching tradition celebration features childrens games, food, and live entertainment and music.

Free Admission   Kid Friendly Event
Hours: 10am - 4pm

8/1/2015 - 8/1/2015
Dirty Face Music Fest
Thousand Trails Campground - Leavenworth, WA
www.iciclearts.org/dirtyface/   (509) 548-2278

Join us for live music, camping, dancing, beers, wines, and family friendly activites all day!

Paid Admission   Kid Friendly Event

Vendor Contact: info@iciclearts.org

8/1/2015 - 8/2/2015
Drayton Harbor Days Festival
Blaine Marina - Blaine, WA
www.blainechamber.com (360) 332-6484

This two-day event celebrates the maritime history of Blaine! Come join us for a variety of family fun activities, including a sail boat race, arts and crafts vendors, kids activities, raft race and much more!

Free Admission
Kid Friendly Event
Hours: 10 am - 5pm

Vendor Contact: vic@cityofblaine.com
# of Vendors: 45 Deadline: 7/15/15
Attendance: 2000

8/1/2015 - 8/29/2015
Ilwaco Saturday Market
Port of Ilwaco - Ilwaco, WA
www.portofilwaco.com (503) 338-9511

Explore the historic fishing village of Ilwaco, picnic on smoked salmon chowder, juicy hamburgers, crunchy kettl corn, hot donts, handmade sausage and a variety of yummy baked boods. Shop for fresh farm produce, and regionally created arts & crafts!

Admission: Not Provided Kid Friendly Event
Hours: 10am - 4pm

Vendor Contact: satmkt.bruce@gmail.com

I love summertime more than anything else in the world. That is the only thing that gets me through the winter... knowing that summer is going to be there.
~~Jack McBrayer, American Actor

8/1/2015 - 8/29/2015
Issaquah Fall Farmers Market
Pickering Barn - Issaquah, WA
www.ci.issaquah.wa.us   (425) 837-3311

Activities for children and families, cooking demos, farm-fresh seasonal fruits and veggies, food vendors, fresch-cut flowers, fresh-baked goods, handmade arts and crafts, mini concerts and entertainment, organic produce and on-site Master Gardner.

Free Admission   Kid Friendly Event
Hours: 9 am - 2 pm

Vendor Contact: Jera Gilmore & Cynthia Wright
issaquahfarmersmarket@issaquahwa.gov
# of Vendors: 130   Juried Event
Attendance: 95,000   # of Years Held: 24

8/1/2015 - 8/1/2015
Port Orchard Summer Artwalk
Downtown - Port Orchard, WA
www.pobsa.com/membership/port-orchard-art-walk.html   (360) 676-3693

Gifts, prizes, local business discounts, raffles and more! Amazing local artists along with music! Enjoy the great art and relax in downtown Port Orchard.

Admission: Not Provided
Hours: 2pm - 5pm

Vendor Contact: Christine Stansbery
portorchardartwalk@gmail.com
# of Vendors: 20

Attendance: 500+

8/1/2015 - 8/1/2015
Proctor Arts Fest
North 26th & Proctor Streets - Tacoma, WA
www.proctorartsfest.com   (253) 752-5200

Featuring 160 arts and crafts vendors, three stages of musical entertainment, family stage, kids area, farmers' market, dog fashion show and parade and a merchants sidewalk sale.

Free Admission   Kid Friendly Event
Hours: 10 am - 5:30 pm

Vendor Contact: Nancy Frederick
nancy@chaletbowl.com
# of Vendors: 160   Juried Event
Deadline: 2/28/15
Attendance: 10000+   # of Years Held: 20

8/1/2015 - 8/1/2015
University Place Sun Fest
Market Square in University Place (36th & Bridgeport Way W) - University Place, WA
www.cityofup.com/residents/events/university-place-sun-fest-formerly-university-place-festival-aug-1

Admission: Not Provided   Kid Friendly Event
Hours: 10am - 5pm

Vendor Contact: joel@ventiproductions.com

8/5/2015 - 8/9/2015
Gray's Harbor County Fair
County Fairgrounds - Grays Harbor, WA
www.ghcfairgrounds.com   (360) 482-2651

Paid Admission
Kid Friendly Event

8/5/2015 - 8/25/2015
Street Tunes
Throughout Everett - Everett, WA
www.everettwa.gov/765/Festivals-Events
(425) 257-7117

You're invited to jam! Street Tunes is an interactive art project from start to finish. The event begins with artists decorating each piano. Pianos are placed on the street for anyone to stop and play a tune, or just tickle the ivories!

Free Admission   Kid Friendly Event

Vendor Contact: Carol Thomas
cthomas@everettwa.gov

8/6/2015 - 8/9/2015
Island County Fair
Island County Fairgrounds - Langley, WA
www.whidbeyislandfair.com   (360) 221-4677

Quality exhibits from the farm, including all types of livestock, local crops, handmade art exhibits, quilting and fiber arts. Fun for all!

Paid Admission   Kid Friendly Event
Hours: Fair gates open at 9:30 am

Vendor Contact: 19icfa12@whidbey.com
# of Vendors: 80

Attendance: 25000
# of Years Held: 91

Summer afternoon—summer afternoon; to me those have always been the two most beautiful words in the English language.
~~Henry James 1843 - 1916

8/6/2015 - 8/9/2015
Pierce County Fair
Frontier Park - Graham, WA
www.piercecountyfair.com   (253) 843-1173

Celebrating our 68th year, come join us for a celebration of rural life, agriculture and good ol' family values! Nestled amount the giant first of beautiful Frontier Park, you'll enjoy tasty fair food, entertainment acts and attractions, livestock shows and exhibits, kids pedal tractor pull, live music, roving entertainment, carnival, arts and crafts, and plenty of kids activities.

Paid Admission   Kid Friendly Event
Hours: Fri: 10am - 10pm;
        Sat: 10am - 10 pm;
        Sun: 10am - 6pm

Vendor Contact: betty328@aol.com
# of Vendors: 120   Deadline: 4/1/15
# of Years Held: 68

8/6/2015 - 8/9/2015
Summer Meltdown Festival
Whitehorse Mountain Amphitheater - Darrington, WA
www.summermeltdownfest.com

Located only 1.5 hours outside of both Seattle and Bellingham, Summer Meltdown Festival is an annual tradition and a favorite way for thousands of Pacific Northwesterners to celebrate summer, the wilds of Washington, and the magic of music underneath Whitehorse Mountain. The festival also features food and crafts, shaded campgrounds, a river, a yoga tent, a beer garden, a kids village, and newly added outdoor adventure activities. STS9, Iration and Tycho headline its biggest lineup yet.

Paid Admission
Kid Friendly Event
# of Years Held: 15

8/7/2015 - 8/9/2015
31st Annual Mt. St. Helens Bluegrass Festival
Toledo High School grounds - Toledo, WA
www.washingtonbluegrassassociation.org
(360) 520-4524

Bluegrass performers: Phillip Steinmetz & His Sunny Tennesseans, Tommy Brown & The County Line Grass, John Kael and Annie Staninec & Whiskey Deaf, Rural Delivery, John Shubert & The Stray Dogs. Family event.

Dry Camping $25 for 3 nights (Thurs/Fri/Sat), Showers. Pets on leash at campsite. $35 - Weekend Pass; $20 - Friday Night Only; $25 - Saturday All Day; FREE Sunday Gospel Concert - 9:30am; FREE - Saturday Workshops - 9:30am. Take exit 63 off Interstate 5

Paid Admission
Hours: Friday: all day
         Saturday: all day Sunday: til Noon.

Vendor Contact: General Cothren
Generalandbetty7@msn.com   Not a Juried Event

# of Years Held: 31

©Harney County Fair – Used With Permission

8/7/2015 - 8/9/2015
Anacortes Arts Festival
Downtown Anacortes - Anacortes, WA
www.anacortesartsfestival.com   (360) 293-6211

Diverse booth artisans will transform six blocks of historic downtown! Extending down to the water, Arts at the Port explores the them, "Air, Earth, Water" with over 40 regional fine artists and youth art exhibition. Hands-on kids activities spark the creativity of the youngest festival-goers! Regional and ethnic foods, wine, bear and spirits are available at three locations. Three stages filled with lively rock, country, jazz and world music will entertainment your family!

Paid Admission
Kid Friendly Event
Hours: Fri & Sat: 10 - 6; Sun: 10 - 5

Vendor Contact: staff@anacortesartsfestival.com
# of Vendors: 250   Juried Event
Attendance: 75000   # of Years Held: 54

8/7/2015 - 8/9/2015
Blue Waters Bluegrass Festival
Waterfront Park - Medical Lake, WA
www.bluewatersbluegrass.org   (509) 951-5468

This event is possibly the best summertime bluegrass festival in the Northwest! Featuring a world-class line-up of performers.

Paid Admission   No Kid's Activities

Vendor Contact: bluewatersbluegrass@yahoo.com
Deadline: 7/17/15

Buttercups in the August sunshine are like little cups of gold,
Dasies and sunflowers rise with bowing head towards the sun,
Violets of majestic blue creep within the shadow of the tree,
Butterflies dance from flower-to-flower,
Fluttering on the summer breeze and never a care in the world.
~~ Catherine Pittman © 2015

8/7/2015 - 8/16/2015
Clark County Fair
Clark County Fairgrounds - Ridgefield, WA
www.clarkcofair.com   (360) 397-6180

Endless entertainment and excitement can be found here! Family activities, carnival midway, Comcast Kids Park, kids stage for kids contests, local entertainment and acts, poiny rides, livestock events and exhibits,. Plenty of family fun!

Paid Admission
Kid Friendly Event

Vendor Contact: ccfair@clarkcofair.com
# of Vendors: 300

8/7/2015 - 8/9/2015
Festival at Mount Si
Si View Metro Park - North Bend, WA
www.festivalatmtsi.org   (425) 888-8535

Preserving the past...celebrate the present...embrace the future! Shop 'til you drop with arts and crafts from vendors all over the state of Washington. Lots of corn-on-the-cob, elephant ears and more great foomd from Washington's best food and drink vendors. Relax in the beer garden, groove to jazz, blues, rock, country and more with live performances on two stages. Kids can bop 'til they drop at their own fun zone. The event begins with the Grand Parade, and ends with spectacular fireworks.

Admission: Not Provided
Kid Friendly Event

Vendor Contact: mrudd@siviewpark.org
# of Vendors: 120   Deadline: 7/25/15
Attendance: 30,000

8/7/2015 - 8/7/2015
Fremont First Friday Art Walk
New Saturn Building - Seattle, WA
www.fremontfirstfriday.com

Neighborhood art supporting shops, galleries and restaurants celebrate creativity in it's many forms. You'll find oil paintings, photography, illustrations, sculpture, mixed media and live musical entertainment!

Admission: Not Provided
No Kid's Activities
Hours: 6pm - 9pm

Vendor Contact: freemontfirstfriday@gmail.com
# of Vendors: 20

8/7/2015 - 8/8/2015
Kirkland Summerfest
Downtown Kirkland - Kirkland, WA
www.kirklandsummerfest.com   (425) 456-1111

Kirkland's premere summer festival is a fun family-frinedly event on the waterfront. Featuring two days of visual and performing arts, kids activities, spectator sports and live entertainment. Over 100 vendors of original arts, kids art exhibition, cardboard boat races, and food trucks on the streets of downtown Kirkland. Bring the family for the day, then dance the night away at the beer garden stage!

Paid Admission
Kid Friendly Event
Hours: 11am - 9pm

Vendor Contact: Kristen Gonzales
# of Vendors: 150
Deadline: 6/30/15

8/7/2015 - 8/9/2015
Marysville Street Festival
Downtown - Marysville, WA
www.marysvillemerchants.com   (360) 653-3538

This marketplacce festival showcases local produce, artisans, musicians and artisans displaying their works and demonstrating their crafts.

Admission: Not Provided
Kid Friendly Event
Hours: Fri: 10am - 8pm;
         Sat: 10am - 6pm; Sun: 10am - 4pm

Vendor Contact: Vicki
marysvillemerchants@hotmail.com
# of Vendors: 90   Juried Event
Deadline: 6/30/15

Attendance: 4000
# of Years Held: 30

8/7/2015 - 8/9/2015
Mount St. Helens Bluegrass Festival
Toledo High School - Toledo, WA
www.washingtonbluegrassassociation.org
(360)785-3478

If you're lookin' for some pickin' or just want to chill and listen to some good bluegrass music, then this event is for you!

Paid Admission
No Kid's Activities
Hours: Fri: 5pm - 10pm;
         Sat: 9am - 10pm; Sun: 9am - 5pm

Vendor Contact: generalandbetty7@msn.com
Attendance: 1000+
# of Years Held: 30

8/7/2015 - 8/9/2015
SalmonFest Seattle
Lake City Community Center - Seattle, WA
www.salmonfestseattle.com   (206) 363-3287

Delight in first class entertainment, handmade crafts, delectable foods and an unparalleled Salmon Bake! You won't find any teepees set-up here, but you will find a entertainment stage and beer garden with outdoor seating for families.

Paid Admission
Kid Friendly Event
Hours: 12pm - 6pm

# of Vendors: 90   Deadline: 7/17/15

Attendance: 6000

8/8/2015 - 8/8/2015
Music & Art in Wright Park
Wright Park - Tacoma, WA
www.sites.google.com/site/mawpfestival/
(253) 591-5330

This festival is a fun family-friendly event filled with music and arts, food trucks and more! Rock-n-roll, pop, alternative, and more!

Admission: Not Provided
Kid Friendly Event

Vendor Contact: mawp.art.vendor.info@gmail.com
# of Vendors: 35   Deadline: 7/31/15

Attendance: 2500

Let us dance in the sun, wearing wild flowers in our hair.
~~Susan Polis Schutz, American Author

8/8/2015 - 8/9/2015
Stillaguamish Festival of the River & Pow Wow
20416 Jordan Rd - Arlington, WA
www.festivaloftheriver.com

A fun event with activities for the entire family! Children storytelling and entertainment, fun zone, rides and activities. The traditional alder salmon bake is delicious! Craft exhibits, logging show and more can be found!

Admission: Not Provided
Kid Friendly Event

Vendor Contact: Tamara Neuffer
tneuffer@stillaguamish.com

# of Years Held: 25

8/9/2015 - 8/9/2015
Festival by the Bay
Downtown - Port Orchard, WA
www.fathomsofun.org   (360) 620-3363

Join in the fun at this annual event! Classic street fair that features food, arts & crafts, sales booths, info booths, activities and games for the kiddies and the adults!

Admission: Not Provided
Kid Friendly Event
Hours: 9am - 4pm

Vendor Contact: Bob Morehouse
bob@fathomsofun.org

Attendance: 30,000

8/12/2015 - 8/15/2015
San Juan County Fair
San Juan County Fairgrounds - Friday Harbor, WA
www.sjcfair.org   (360) 378-4310

San Juan County Fair is where the islands come together to celebrate the traditions and talents of their communities! Plenty of fun for the entire family! See livestock 4-H shows, exhibits, eat great food, join the talent contests, hear great live entertainment, and there's plenty of kids activities and more!

Paid Admission
Kid Friendly Event

Vendor Contact: Jennifer Jennifer@sjcfair.org

8/12/2015 - 8/15/2015
Skagit County Fair
Skagit County Fairgrounds - Mount Vernon, WA
www.skagitcounty.net   (360) 675-2277

This award-winning fair is fun for the whole family! Great "hometown fun with a homegrown feel!" Great local entertainment, a carnival, farm animals, displays, kid zone and more events!

Paid Admission
Kid Friendly Event
Hours: 10am - 10pm

# of Vendors: 100

Attendance: 35,000
# of Years Held: 117

8/12/2015 - 8/16/2015
Skamania County Fair & Timber Carnival
Skamania County Fairgrounds - Stevenson, WA
www.skamaniacounty.org   (509) 427-3979

The original "free-gate" fair in the Northwest includes livestock, 4-H fun, delicious food, and a treasure trove of exhibits. Don't miss out on the exciting entertainment, contests, demos, annual parade, timber carnival, market sale and finish the event with the fireworks!

Admission: Not Provided
Kid Friendly Event

Vendor Contact: jackson@co.skamania.wa.us

8/14/2015 - 8/16/2015
14th Great Northwest Nationals
Spokane Fair & Expo Center - Spokane, WA
www.good-guys.com   (925) 218-9151

Custom and classic cars, muscle cars and trucks, hot rods, vendors, live music and more! Thousands of tricked-out cars and trucks!

Paid Admission
Hours: Fri: 8am - 5pm;
         Sat: 8am - 8pm; Sun: 8am - 3pm

Vendor Contact: sales@good-guys.com

Attendance: 30,000
# of Years Held: 14

Every time I see a rainbow, I find a friend beneath its bright glow. Together we watch with wondrous eyes, the wee leprechaun paint and color the skies! So whenever a storm passes you, look for the rainbow and leprechauns too! And if you should stand 'neath its light with a friend, then you've found the gold at the reainbow's end!
~~ Lyrics The Pot of Gold by Catherine Pittman © 1994 from the Album Topsy Toddler Time

8/14/2015 - 8/16/2015
A Taste of Edmonds
Civic Playfield - Edmonds, WA
www.atasteofedmonds.com   (425) 489-7900

This 3-day festival is filled with fun music, great food, other entertainment performance and thrilling rides. It's a great time fot the entire family!

Paid Admission
Kid Friendly Event
Hours: Fri & Sat: 11am - 10m;
          Sun: 11am - 7pm

Vendor Contact: Craig Cooke
craig@pacificrimtalent.com
# of Vendors: 200   Juried Event
Deadline: 5/1/15

Attendance: 90,000   # of Years Held: 33

8/14/2015 - 8/16/2015
Auburn Good Ol' Days
Downtown Auburn - Auburn, WA
www.auburndays.com
(253) 939-3389

Bring the family and spend time down at Young 'Uns Square! Plenty of free activities to keep the little ones busy, as well as a variety of performance entertainment throughout the weekend. Stroll down the arts and crafts lane, and check out the wares from skilled artistic folks in the area!

Admission: Not Provided
Kid Friendly Event

Vendor Contact: office@eventheadquartersinc.com
# of Vendors: 120   Juried Event

Attendance: 40,000   # of Years Held: 29

8/14/2015 - 8/16/2015
Bainbridge Island Summer Studio
Various Studios Around Bainbridge Island
Bainbridge Island, WA
www.bistudiotour.com   (206) 842-0504

This outdoor art show features local artists in a garden setting with live music that creates an inviting marketplace of fine art.

Admission: Not Provided
No Kid's Activities
Hours: 10am - 6pm daily

Vendor Contact: Dinah Satterwhite
bistudiotour@earthlink.net
# of Vendors: 65   Juried Event
Deadline: 4/15/15

Attendance: 4000
# of Years Held: 15

8/14/2015 - 8/14/2015
Bothell Farmers Market Kids Day
Country Village Shops - Bothell, WA
www.countryvillagebothell.com/bothell-farmers-market   (425) 483-2250

Free Admission
Kid Friendly Event
Hours: Every Friday, noon - 6pm

Bluegrass has brought more people together and made more friends than any music in the world. You meet people at festivals and renew acquaintances year after year.
~~ Bill Monroe, Musician

8/14/2015 - 8/16/2015
Jefferson County Fair
Jefferson County Fairgrounds - Port Townsend, WA
www.jeffcofairgrounds.com   (360) 385-1013

An old fashioned country Fair with fun for the whole family. Lots of free entertainment: Mud Drags, Draft Horse Pulls, Lace & Lead, Olson Bro Band and much much more! Beef & Salmon BBQ's, 4-H & FFA exhibits Walk On Water. Free Parking   Admission Adults $8.00, Srs/Students $6 5 & under free

Paid Admission
Kid Friendly Event
Hours: Fri & Sat 10am-9pm Sun 10am-6pm

Vendor Contact: Sue McIntire
jeffcofairgrounds@olypen.com
# of Vendors: 120   Not a Juried Event
Deadline: 8/1/15

Attendance: 12000
# of Years Held: 78

8/14/2015 - 8/16/2015
Lake Chelan Fine Arts Festival
Riverwalk Park - Chelan, WA
www.methowarts.org   (509) 682-9781

Held in the heart of the summer when Lake Chelan is at its best! Visitors will enjoy Fine Arts and Fine Crafts on display and for sale. Festival includes culinary arts, fine arts, traditional arts and crafts, live entertainment, food and a kid's castle and art center.

Admission: Not Provided
Kid Friendly Event

Vendor Contact: lakechelanarts@gmail.com
Juried Event   Deadline: 4/20/15
# of Years Held: 6

8/14/2015 - 8/16/2015
Snoqualmie Railroad Days
Historic Downtown - Snoqualmie, WA
www.railroaddays.com   (425) 888-3030

What child doesn't love trains? This annual community event celebrates the spirit and origins of the railroad and logging town, the home of the Snoqualmie Indian Tribe. The annual event features entertainment stages, vendors, grand parade, children's field of fun, timber sports, food and drink venues as well as the Fireman's Pancake Breakfast.

Artisans display and sell their handmade wares, while the Legends Classic Car Club hosts hundreds of classic vehicles. Train excursions will whisk you to the top of Snoqualmie Falls and beyond for a panoramic view of the valley.

Admission: Not Provided
Kid Friendly Event
Hours: Fri: 5pm - 9pm;
            Sat: 7am - 10pm; Sun: 10am - 4pm

# of Vendors: 75   Juried Event
Deadline: 6/30/15

Attendance: 10000
# of Years Held: 77

When an American says that he loves his country, he means not only that he loves the New England hills, the prairies glistening in the sun, the wide and rising plains, the great mountains and the sea. He means that he loves an inner air, an inner light in which freedom lives and in which a man can draw the breath of self-respect.
~~ Adlai Stevenson II, American Statesman
1900 – 1965

8/15/2015 - 8/15/2015
Celebrate Woodinville
17301 131st Avenue NE - Woodinville, WA
www.celebratewoodinville.com   (425) 481-8300

Celebrate Woodinville is a free, community event where enjoy great music, wine, and food. You€™re invited to bring a picnic or purchase food from local restaurants. The wine and beer garden will feature wines from premiere Woodinville Wine Country wineries and craft beer from local breweries. The festival begins with the annual pancake breakfast and Woodinville parade, followed by the Woodinville farmer's market, arts and crafts fair, exhibitors, children's activities, and the popular Bassett Bash.

Free Admission   Kid Friendly Event
Hours: 8am - 6pm

Vendor Contact: Jeanie Rash
events@woodinvillechamber.org
# of Vendors: 25   Not a Juried Event
Deadline: 6/30/15

Attendance: 5000+   # of Years Held: 3

8/15/2015 - 8/16/2015
Conconully Outdoor Quilt & Craft Show
Main St & Silver St - Conconully, WA
www.conconully.com   (509) 826-2241

A fun-filled day in Conconully! Handmade quilts will be on display and for sale. Local and out-of-town crafters will exhibit their handmade works. Food, raffles and music too!

Admission: Not Provided
Hours: 9am - 4pm

Vendor Contact:
outdoorquiltandcraftshow@gmail.com

8/15/2015 - 8/15/2015
Everett Craft Beer Festival
Entrance on Hewitt Ave & Hoyt Ave
Everett, WA 98201 - Everett, WA
www.washingtonbeer.com
(206) 795-5510

The 4th Annual Everett Craft Beer Festival will feature 30 Washington breweries pouring more than 100 beers. To highlight the creativity of our Washington brewers, many beers will be poured through randalls filled with unique ingredients.

Paid Admission   No Kid's Activities
Hours: Saturday, Noon-7pm

# of Vendors: 30 breweries
Attendance: 3000   # of Years Held: 4

8/15/2015 - 8/16/2015
Festival of Artists
Port of Everett Marina - Everett, WA
www.schack.org   (425) 257-8380

Purchase art fresh off the easel as the promenade will be filled with artists at work, turning the marina into one huge outdoor studio and sidewalk gallery! 90+ artists will share their works of painting, pottery, glass, jewelry, photography and more! Glassblowing on site and children's activities can be found at this annual event.

Admission: Not Provided
Kid Friendly Event
Hours: 10am - 5pm daily

Vendor Contact: Maren Oates
# of Vendors: 90   Juried Event
Deadline: 4/24/15
Attendance: 12000
# of Years Held: 20

8/15/2015 - 8/15/2015
Olalla Bluegrass & Beyond Festival
South Kitsap Southern Little League Field, Olalla, WA - Olalla, WA
www.olallabluegrass.com   253 - 857 -5604

Kick the City off Your Shoes(tm) at the 24th-ever Olalla Bluegrass & Beyond Festival! Food & craft vendors, old time craft demonstrations, lots of kids activities (including a parade!), berry pie contest and some of the best bluegrass -and - beyond music you'll hear anywhere. Family friendly, inter-generational, drug-and alcohol-free event. Bands include Eclectic Cloggers, Fern Hill, Bryan Bowers, Blackberry Bushes and Surf Monkey (blues from Seattle).

Paid Admission
Kid Friendly Event
Hours: 11am-8:30pm

Vendor Contact: Larry Davis ldavissped@yahoo.com
# of Vendors: 20   Juried Event
Deadline: 7/14/15

Attendance: 1500
# of Years Held: 24

Vintage Bi-plane © Nightowl All Free Downloads

8/15/2015 - 8/16/2015
Outdoor Quilt and Craft Show
Main Street and Silver Street - Conconully , WA
www.conconully.com   206-954-2747

Conconully Chamber of Commerce once again hosts their Outdoor Quilt and Craft Show in our small mountain town 21 miles out of Omak and Okanogan,WA. Featuring handmade quilts for show and sale, and heirloom quilts on display in the museum yard.

If you are a quilter and would like to display or sell your quilts, we are a show you won't want to miss!   Along with the quilts we have venders who sell their American handmade works. We look forward to having you register or attend our event.   Information & registration forms are online at Conconully.com under Events.

Free Admission
No Kid's Activities
Hours: S-S 9am-4pm

Vendor Contact: Janet Warner
Outdoorquiltandcraftshow@gmail.com
# of Vendors: 160   Not a Juried Event
Deadline: 8/1/15
Attendance: 2000   # of Years Held: 2

8/15/2015 - 8/16/2015
Seattle Street Food Festival
South Lake Union - Seattle, WA
www.mobilefoodrodeo.com

Admission: Not Provided
No Kid's Activities
Hours: Sat: 12pm - 10pm; Sun: 11am - 7pm

Vendor Contact: vendors@piranhablonde.com
# of Vendors: 75   Attendance: 145,000

8/15/2015 - 8/15/2015
Uptown Crafts Fair
Port Townsend Community Center - Port Townsend, WA
www.porttownsendartsguild.org   (360) 774-6544

Admission: Not Provided
Hours: 10am - 5pm

Vendor Contact: Donna Harding & Jess Hogan
ptartsguild@yahoo.com
# of Vendors: 45   Juried Event
Attendance: 5000

8/15/2015 - 8/16/2015
Westport Art Festival
WestportMarina & Museum - Westport, WA
www.westportartfestival.org   (360) 268-1825

Enjoy artisans handcrafted wares, great food plus Discovery Days for the kids that features nature-based craft projeccts and free entertainment throughout the festival!

Admission: Not Provided
Kid Friendly Event

Vendor Contact: Joan Hulsinga
joanheart@techline.com
# of Vendors: 80   Juried Event
Deadline: 7/25/15

Attendance: 5000

There is nothing in the world so much like prayer as music is.
~~William P Merrill, American Presbyterian Clergyman
1867- 1954

8/17/2015 - 8/22/2015
Northwest Washington Fair
Fairgrounds - Lynden, WA
www.nwwafair.com

Admission: Not Provided
Kid Friendly Event

Vendor Contact: Jim Baron
# of Vendors: 200
Deadline: 6/15/15

Attendance: 180000

8/18/2015 - 8/22/2015
Grant County Fair
Grant County Fairgrounds - Moses Lake, WA
www.gcfairgounds.com

Admission: Not Provided
Kid Friendly Event

Vendor Contact:
grantcountyfairgrounds@co.grant.wa.us
# of Vendors: 250

# of Years Held: 104

8/20/2015 - 8/23/2015
Clallam County Fair
Fairgrounds - Port Angeles, WA
www.clallam.net/fair/

Admission: Not Provided
Kid Friendly Event

Vendor Contact: fairgrounds@co.clallam.wa.us
# of Vendors: 150

Attendance: 30000

8/20/2015 - 8/23/2015
Northeast Washington Fair
NE Washington Fairgrounds - Colville, WA
www.co.stevens.wa.us

Admission: Not Provided
Kid Friendly Event

Vendor Contact: Lori Matlock
lmatlock@co.stevens.wa.us
# of Vendors: 60   Deadline: 7/1/15

Attendance: 15000

8/21/2015 - 8/22/2015
Highland Community Days
Tieton Square - Tieton, WA
www.cityoftieton.com   (509) 728-5953

Admission: Not Provided

Native American Dance
© *Michelle Walters* All Free Downloads

8/21/2015 - 8/22/2015
National Lentil Festival
Pullman, Wa - Pullman, WA
www.lentilfest.com
800-365-6948

Lentil Fest is a FREE two-day event in Pullman, WA and includes live cooking demos, the Legendary Lentil Cook-off, food and vendor marketplace, live music by many artists including Dylan Scott, Austin Jenckes and more. The event also includes a wine and beer garden, sporting events like a 5K and a fun kids area.

Free Admission
Kid Friendly Event
Hours: Friday, 5-11pm Saturday, 7:30am-5pm

Vendor Contact: Alexandria Anderson
events@pullmanchamber.com
# of Vendors: 120   Deadline: 6/12/15

Attendance: 30,000
# of Years Held: 27

8/22/2015 - 8/23/2015
Find Yer' Treasure Gift Fair
Ocean Shores Convention Center - Ocean Shores, WA
www.gpsfundraisersandevents.com

Admission: Not Provided
Kid Friendly Event

Vendor Contact:
gpsfundraisersandevents@gmail.com

8/22/2015 - 8/23/2015
Harvest Festival
Camlann Village - 10320 Kelly Rd NE - Carnation, WA
www.camlann.org   (425) 788-8624

Paid Admission   Kid Friendly Event

8/26/2015 - 8/30/2015
Kitsap County Fair & Stampede
Kitsap County Fairgrounds and Events Center
Bremerton, WA
www.thebigcountyfair.com   (360) 337-5350

The 2015 Kitsap County Fair & Stampede is right around the corner, August 26-30, 2015! Xtreme Bulls are back on Wednesday August 26th at 7pm! PRCA Rodeo nightly 7pm August 27-29, 2015!   D-Derby Sunday August 30th! Food, Carnival, Exhibits, Vendors, entertainment! HAY! It's Kitsap Fair & Stampede Time!

Paid Admission
Kid Friendly Event
Hours: Wed-Sat 10am to 10pm
          Sun 10am to 6pm Carnival opens daily at 11am

Vendor Contact: Fair Info fairinfo@co.kitsap.wa.us
# of Vendors: 250   Not a Juried Event
Deadline: Now

Attendance: 77000
# of Years Held: 71

8/27/2015 - 9/7/2015
Evergreen State Fair
Fairgrounds - Monroe, WA
www.evergreenfair.org   (360) 805-6705

Admission: Not Provided
Kid Friendly Event

Attendance: 880,000

A man's country is not a certain area of land, of mountains, rivers and woods, but it is a principle; and patriotism is loyalty to that principle.
~~ George William Curtis, American Writer 1824 – 1892

8/28/2015 - 8/30/2015
Chehalis Garlic Fest & Craft Show
Southwest Washington Fairgrounds - Chehalis, WA
www.chehalisgarlicfest.com   (360) 748-6836

Admission: Not Provided
Hours: Fi: 12pm-8pm; Sat: 10am-8pm; Sun: 10am-4pm

Vendor Contact: Judy DeVaul
jdevaul@theadvocateagency.com
# of Vendors: 85   Juried Event

Attendance: 15000
# of Years Held: 19

8/29/2015 - 8/29/2015
South Sound Craft Beer Festival
2727 E D St Tacoma, WA 98421 -
Tacoma , WA
www.washingtonbeer.com
(206) 795-5510

The 2nd annual South Sound Craft Beer Festival will feature 30 Washington breweries pouring over 100 craft beers. Our Washington brewers will be featuring a PNW farotite, the IPA, during two tasting sessions at the Tacoma Dome Exhibition Hall.

Paid Admission
No Kid's Activities
Hours: Saturday, August 29, 2015

# of Vendors: 30 breweries
Attendance: 2000
# of Years Held: 2

8/29/2015 - 8/29/2015
Wizard Fest
Country Village Shops - Bothell, WA
www.countryvillagebothell.com/wizard-fest-0

Put on your cape and grab your magical wand for a day full of enchantment and magic! Wizard shows, wizard quests, fantasy authors and magical vendors.

Free Admission - Some Activities are Paid
Kid Friendly Event   Hours: 11am - 5pm

Swan Swimming
on a Lake
Watercolor
© Leslie Pittman

O beautiful for spacious skies,
For amber waves of grain.
For purple mountains majesties,
Above the fruited plain!
America! America! God shed his grace on thee,
And crown thy good with brother hood,
From sea to shining sea!
~~ Lyrics – America the Beautiful
Words by katharine Lee Bates; Melody by Samuel Ward

9/2/2015 - 9/7/2015
Pig Out in the Park
Riverfront Park - Spokane, WA
www.spokanepigout.com   (509) 921-5579

Pig Out is Spokane's favorite annual food and entertainment festival. The six-day festival is open FREE to the public. Featuring 45 great food booths, thre beverage gardens for adults and 100 free concerts on three stages.

Free Admission   Kid Friendly Event

Vendor Contact: billme123@comcast.net
# of Years Held: 36

9/3/2015 - 9/7/2015
Kittlas County Fair
Kittlas County Fairgrounds - Ellensburg, WA
www.kittlascountyfair.com   (509) 952-7639

An old-fashioned fair with fun for everyone! Food, games entertainment contests, judged exhibits and lots of livestock. Come experience the sounds, smells,tastes and memories being made at the county fair!

Admission: Not Provided   Kid Friendly Event
Hours: Thurs - Sun: 10am - 10pm; Mon: 10am - 6pm

# of Vendors: 85   Deadline: 8/1/15
Attendance: 70000

Autumn is the hush before winter.
~~ French Proverb

9/3/2015 - 9/6/2015
Okanogan County Fair
Okanogan County Fairgrounds - Okanogan, WA
www.okanoganfair.org   (509) 322-1621

Admission: Not Provided
Kid Friendly Event

Vendor Contact: fair@co.okanogan.wa.us
# of Vendors: 120

Attendance: 20000
# of Years Held: 68

9/4/2015 - 9/6/2015
Oak Harbor Music Festival
Historic Downtown - Oak Harbor, WA
www.oakharborfestival.com

Admission: Not Provided
Kid Friendly Event

Vendor Contact: info@oakharborfestival.com
# of Vendors: 40

Attendance: 3000

9/4/2015 - 9/6/2015
Walla Walla Fair & Frontier Days
Walla Walla County Fairgrounds - Walla Walla, WA
www.wallawallafair.com   (509) 527-3247

Admission: Not Provided
Kid Friendly Event

# of Vendors: 200

Attendance: 80000
# of Years Held: 147

9/5/2015 - 9/5/2015
69th Annual Seafood Festival & Craft Show
Westport, WA   www.westportwa.com

Admission: Not Provided

9/5/2015 - 9/7/2015
Bremerton Blackberry Festival
Downtown - Bremerton, WA
www.blackberryfestival.org   (360) 377-3041

Admission: Not Provided
Kid Friendly Event
Hours: Sat: 10am-7pm;
             Sun: 10am - 6pm; Mon: 10am - 5pm

Vendor Contact: Carol Atkinson
# of Vendors: 165   Deadline: 6/10/15

Attendance: 50000
# of Years Held: 26

...To lie sometimes on the grass under the trees on a summer's day, listening to the murmur of water, or watching the clouds float across the blue sky, is by no means waste of time.
~~John Lubbock, "Recreation," The Use of Life, 1894

...September is dressing herself in showy dahlias and splendid marigolds and starry zinnias.
~~Oliver Wendel Holmes, Poet 1809-1894

Fall has always been my favorite season. The time when everything bursts with its last beauty, as if nature had been saving up all year for the grand finale. ~~ Lauren DeStefano, Author from her book, Wither

A painter paints pictures on a blank canvas;
nature paints pictures on the seasons.
~~ Catherine Pittman © 201

9/5/2015 - 9/5/2015
Leavenworth Lions Craft Fair
Lions Club Park - Leavenworth, WA
www.Leavenworth-Lions-Craft-Fair.weebly.com
(509) 860-0355

Join us Saturday, September 5th, 2015 from 10am - 4pm in beautiful Leavenworth Washington for our 2nd Annual Craft Fair. The craft fair will be held in Leavenworth Lions Park and the weather will be perfect! Great gifts for any occasion. Light breakfast and lunch service will be available in the park during craft fair hours. All proceeds go to Leavenworth Lions' Service Projects for our community. Please visit our website at http://Leavenworth-Lions-Craft-Fair.weebly.com to view vendors and products. You may also email us at 2015LeavenworthCraftFair@gmail.com

Free Admission
Hours: Saturday, 10am - 4pm

Vendor Contact: Leavenworth Lions Club
2015LeavenworthLionsCraftFair@gmail.com
# of Vendors: 71   Juried Event
Deadline: 8/10/15

Attendance: 300 - 500
# of Years Held: 2

9/5/2015 - 9/5/2015
Port Orchart Art Walk
Downtown - Port Orchard, WA
(360) 676-3693

Admission: Not Provided   No Kid's Activities
Hours: 2pm - 5pm

Vendor Contact: Christine Stansbery
portorchardartwalk@gmail.com
# of Vendors: 20   Attendance: 500

9/5/2015 - 9/6/2015
Roy Fall Pioneer Rodeo
8710 Higgins Greig Rd - Roy, WA
www.royrodeo.com

Admission: Not Provided
Vendor Contact: roy_rodeo@hotmail.com

9/5/2015 - 9/5/2015
Westport Seafood Festival
Maritime Museum - Westport, WA
www.westportgrayland-chamber.org
(360) 267-6107

Admission: Not Provided
Kid Friendly Event
Hours: 11am - 6pm

Attendance: 2000
# of Years Held: 67

9/11/2015 - 9/13/2015
Mukilteo Lighthouse Festival
Lighthouse Park - Mukilteo, WA
www.mukilteolighthousefestival.com
(425) 353-5516

Admission: Not Provided
Kid Friendly Event
Hours: Fri: 3pm - 7pm;
        Sat: 11am - 7pm; Sun: 11am - 5pm

Vendor Contact: info@mukilteofestival.org
# of Vendors: 50   # of Years Held: 50

---

*I am summer, come to lure you away from your
computer...Come dance on my fresh grass, dig your toes into
my beaches.
~~Oriana Green, @NatureSpirits*

9/11/2015 - 9/13/2015
Ocean Shores Arts & Crafts Festival
Ocean Shores Convention Center - Ocean Shores, WA
www.associatedarts.org   (360) 289-9586

Admission: Not Provided
Kid Friendly Event
Hours: Fri: 12pm-5pm;
        Sat: 10am-6pm; Sun: 10am-4pm

Vendor Contact: Helen Lord info@associatedarts.org
# of Vendors: 120

Attendance: 10000
# of Years Held: 48

9/11/2015 - 9/20/2015
Spokane County Interstate Fair
Spokane County Fair & Expo Center
Spokane Valley, WA
www.spokanecounty.org/fairs/slf/
(509) 477-1766

Admission: Not Provided
Kid Friendly Event

Vendor Contact: rbuchanan@spokanecounty.org
# of Vendors: 200

Attendance: 200000

9/11/2015 - 9/13/2015
Westport Blues Festival
Westport Inn - Westport, WA
www.westportblues.com   (360) 268-0715

Admission: Not Provided

9/11/2015 - 9/13/2015
Wooden Boat Festival
Point Hudson marina - Port Townsend, WA

Regattas, Sailing, craft demos, boat building and more.

Admission: Not Provided

Vendor Contact: Bart Trailer/Carrie Muellner
# of Vendors: 70   Not a Juried Event
Deadline: 6/15/15

Attendance: 35000

9/12/2015 - 9/14/2015
Art in the Park
Pioneer Park - Ferndale, WA
www.cityofferndale.org   (360) 410-0918

Free Admission

Vendor Contact: ferndalearts@cityofferndale.org
Deadline: 6/17/15
# of Years Held: 3

9/12/2015 - 9/13/2015
Crafts by the Dock
Downtown - Port Townsend, WA
www.porttownsendartsguild.org   (360) 774-6544

Admission: Not Provided
Hours: Sat: 10am - 6pm; Sun: 10am - 5pm

Vendor Contact: Donna Harding & Jess Hogan
ptartsguild@yahoo.com
# of Vendors: 56   Juried Event

Attendance: 5000

9/12/2015 - 9/13/2015
Kelso Highlander Festival and Scottish Games
Tam O'Shanter Park - Kelso, WA
www.kelso.gov/visitors/highlander-festival
(360) 423-0900

Kelso Highlander Festival Invites you to come and experience a "Wee Bit O'™ Scotland"□ September 12th & 13th.Come experience the Highland Dance Competition, Highland Team Games, Heavyweight Events, Fun Run/Walk, Bagpipe Bands, Scottish Vendors, Food, Avenue of the Clans, Scone Baking Contest, Silent Auction, Parade, Arm Wrestling Contest. Entertainment by: the Wicked Tinkers and Men of Worth.

Free Admission
Kid Friendly Event
Hours: Saturday and Sunday, from 9 to 5 pm.

Attendance: 6000
# of Years Held: 31

9/12/2015 - 9/12/2015
Night Market & Moon Festival
International District - Seattle, WA
www.mobilefoodrodeo.com

Admission: Not Provided
Kid Friendly Event

Vendor Contact: vendors@piranhablonde.com
# of Years Held: 7

Summer afternoon—summer afternoon; to me those have always been the two most beautiful words in the English language.
~~Henry James 1843 - 1916

9/12/2015 – 9/12/2015
Skagit River Salmon Festival
Waterfront Park at Swinomish
Casino & Lodge - Anacortes, WA
www.skagitriverfest.org
(360) 542-7912

Join us for SPAWNtaneous fun as we celebrate the Skagit River and return of the salmon. The Festival features youth activities, artisans, recreational and educational booths, music, great food, raptor shows, Puget Sound DockDogs competition, Native American music and storytellers. Live music is featured all day. W

atch the Hunters of the Sky raptor program and see these amazing birds up close. In the colorful salmon tent, storytellers will spin tales for young and old alike.

Free Admission
Kid Friendly Event
Hours: Saturday, 10 a.m. - 7 p.m.

Vendor Contact: Sarah Nelson
skagitriverfest@gmail.com
# of Vendors: 20   Juried Event
Deadline: 7/13/15

Attendance: 6,000+
# of Years Held: 3

Oh, the summer night,
Has a smile of light,
And she sits on a sapphire throne.
~~ Barry Cornwall, English Poet 1787-1874

9/12/2015 - 9/13/2015
Snohomish Pumpkin Hurl & Medieval Faire
43rd Ave SE and Ebey Island Road - Everett, Washington
www.festivalofpumpkins.org

Watch pumpkins fly & die and Armored Warriors battle it out!

Trebuchets and other launching devices hurl pumpkins! On Saturday, it's a crazy competition! On Sunday it's All Chunkers Welcome: bring and demo your chunkin device just for fun, or get a chance to launch a pumpkin with our air cannon or man-powered trebuchets.

See mounted knights battle on horseback & play in our medieval village both days! Try tasty treats in our food-truck village too! Hands on demos, fall fun & more!

Paid Admission   Kid Friendly Event
Hours: Saturday & Sunday 10:00 am - 4:00 pm

Vendor Contact: Debbie Carlson Gould
manager@festivalofpumpkins.org
# of Vendors: indefinite   Juried Event
Deadline: 8/25/15

Attendance: 4000
# of Years Held: 7

Autumn Still Life
© David Wagner
All Free
Downloads

9/12/2015 - 9/13/2015
Tacoma Fall Wedding Expo
Tacoma Dome - Tacoma, WA
www.bridesclub.com/wedding-expos
425-922-7924

The Tacoma Fall Wedding Expo is the largest south Puget Sound expo of its kind and the perfect place to meet face to face with top wedding professionals to get all the help you need to plan your dream wedding.

Paid Admission
Kid Friendly Event
Hours: Saturday 9:30 am - 4 pm
            Sunday 10:30 am - 4 pm

Vendor Contact: Brad Buckles brad@bridesclub.com
# of Vendors: 150   Deadline: 9/1/15

9/18/2015 - 9/20/2015
Deutschesfest Street Fair
Odessa, Washington - Odessa, WA
www.Odessachamber.net   (509) 988-0430

Odessa celebrates its German Heritage during the annual Deutschesfest celebration. The Street Fair features 30-40 vendors. Vendor spaces start at 10 x 10 feet, and can be as long as 10 x 40 feet. Spaces are $50 for the first and $25 for each additional space. It is estimated that 10,000 people visit the small community to enjoy the food and Bier Garten each year.

Paid Admission
Kid Friendly Event
Hours: Friday and Saturday, 10am-7pm
            Sunday, September 20 11am-2pm

Vendor Contact: Terri King kingt@odessa.wednet.edu
# of Vendors: unlimited   Deadline: 9/10/15

Attendance: 1000   # of Years Held: 40

9/18/2015 - 9/18/2015
Great Wallingford Wurst Festival
St. Benedict School - Seattle, WA
www.stbens.net   (206) 545-1643

Admission: Not Provided
Kid Friendly Event

Vendor Contact: jsmbrose@aol.com
# of Vendors: 45

Attendance: 10000
# of Years Held: 30

9/18/2015 - 9/20/2015
Oktoberfest Monroe
Evergreen State Fairgrounds - Monroe, WA
www.oktoberfestmonroe.com   (425) 295-3262

Admission: Not Provided
Kid Friendly Event
Hours: Fri: Noon-midnight;
             Sat: 11am - midnight; Sun: 11am - 6pm

Vendor Contact: Jody jodym@festivals-inc.com
# of Vendors: 10

Attendance: 5000
# of Years Held: 3

9/19/2015 - 9/19/2015
Bigfoot Bash & Bounty
Home Valley Park - Home Valley, WA
www.facebook.com/pages/Bigfoot-Bash-and-
Bounty/54590278425   (800) 989-9178

Admission: Not Provided
Vendor Contact: info@skamania.org

9/19/2015 - 9/20/2015
Everett Fall Wedding Expo
Xfinity Arena - Everett, WA
www.bridesclub.com/wedding-expos
425-922-7924

Bring your girlfriends and meet top wedding professionals from your area and plan your perfect wedding!

Paid Admission   Kid Friendly Event
Hours: Saturday 10am-4pm Sunday 11am-4pm

Vendor Contact: Brad Buckles brad@bridesclub.com
# of Vendors: 85   Deadline: 9/1/15

9/19/2015 - 9/19/2015
Northwest Homesteading Fair
Lyle Activity Center & Greenspace - Lyle, WA
www.nwhomesteadingfair.wordpress.com/

Free Admission
Kid Friendly Event

Vendor Contact: nwhfvendors@gmail.com
Deadline: 9/16/15
# of Years Held: 4

9/19/2015 - 9/19/2015
Pirate Day
Country Village Shops - Bothell, WA
www.countryvillagebothell.com/pirate-day-2

Arrrggg! Put on your pirate garb and follow the clues on a treasure map to solve a mystery! Meet the Pirates of Treasure Island (noon - 3pm) too!

Free Admission
Kid Friendly Event
Hours: Noon - 4pm

9/19/2015 - 9/20/2015
Seattle Mini-Maker Faire
EMP Museum - Seattle, WA
www.makerfaireseattle.com

Paid Admission

Vendor Contact: makerfaire@EMPmuseum.org
# of Vendors: 70
Deadline: 7/1/15

Attendance: 6000

9/23/2015 - 10/31/2015
Carpinito Brothers' Pumpkin Patch, Corn Maze &
Farm Fun Yard
Carpinito Farms 6868 S 277th St - Lemt, WA
www.carpinto.com   (253) 854-5692

Hayrides, corn mazes, farm fun yard, and pumpkins galore! Concession stand includes hot roasted corn, fresh popped kettle corn, frankfurter sausages, hot and cold drinks.

Admission: Not Provided   Kid Friendly Event
Vendor Contact: info@carpinito.com

9/25/2015 - 10/4/2015
Central Washington State Fair
Fairgrounds - Yakima, WA
www.statefairpark.org/p/central-wa-state-fair
(509) 248-7160, ext. 117

Paid Admission   Kid Friendly Event

# of Vendors: 350
Attendance: 320000

9/25/2015 - 9/27/2015
Everett Fall Home Show
Xfinity Arena - Everett, WA
www.everettfallhomeshow.com   (206) 248-8430

Everett Fall Home Show, Xfinity Arena. The largest
home show between Seattle and the Canadian Border!

Paid Admission   No Kid's Activities
Hours: Friday, noon to 7pm Saturday, 10 to 7pm
            Sunday, 10 to 5pm

Vendor Contact: Bill Bradley bbwestlake@seanet.com
# of Vendors: 425   Not a Juried Event

Attendance: 15 to 20,000   # of Years Held: 12

9/25/2015 - 9/27/2015
Everett Gift Show
Xfinity Arena - Everett, WA
www.everettfallhomeshow.com   (206) 248-8430

Everett Gift Show Xfinity Arena. All types of commercial
and non-commercial items!

Paid Admission
No Kid's Activities
Hours: Fri: Noon - 7pm; Sat & Sun: 10am-7pm,

Vendor Contact: Bill Bradley bbwestlake@seanet.com
# of Vendors: 225   Not a Juried Event

Attendance: 12.000 TO 15,000
# of Years Held: 11

Let us dance in the sun, wearing wild flowers in our hair.
~~Susan Polis Schutz, American Author

9/25/2015 - 9/27/2015
Valleyfest
Mirabeau Point Park & Center
Place Regional Event Center -
Spokane Valley, WA
www.valleyfest.org   (509) 922-3299

Valleyfest---Spokane Valley's premier community event, an annual tradition bringing the community together since 1990. Live entertainment on 3 different stages, the opportunity to have fun with friends, and recognize area youth for their talents. Our "Hearts of Gold" parade kicks off ValleyFest Friday night, followed on Saturday and Sunday with various booths and vendors in the park and other fun family events.

Admission: Not Provided   Kid Friendly Event
Hours: See event schedule online

Vendor Contact: info@valleyfest.org

9/25/2015 - 9/27/2015
Washington State Autumn Leaf Festival
Downtown Leavenworth - Leavenworth, WA
www.autumnleaffestival.com

Admission: Not Provided

Vendor Contact: autumnleaffestival@outlook.com
Deadline: 9/1/15

9/26/2015 - 9/27/2015
Bellevue Wedding Expo
Bellevue Hilton - Bellevue, WA
www.bridesclub.com   (425) 455-1300

Admission: Not Provided
No Kid's Activities
Hours: Sat: 10am - 4pm; Sun: 11am - 4pm

9/26/2015 - 10/31/2015
Craven Farm's Fall Festival & Corn Maze
Craven Farm - Snohomish, WA

Admission: Not Provided

9/28/2015 - 9/30/2015
Newport Music Festival
City Park - Newport, WA
www.pvbluegrass.com   (509) 675-6590

Admission: Not Provided
No Kid's Activities

Vendor Contact: Mark Mark@pvbluegrass.com
# of Vendors: 25

Attendance: 1000   # of Years Held: 9

---

*The sea does not reward those who are too anxious, too greedy
or too impatient. One should lie empty, open, choiceless as a
beach- waiting for a gift from the sea.*
~~ Anne Morrow Lindbergh, American Author 1906 – 2001

*The three great elemental sounds in nature are the sound of
rain, the sound of wind in a primeval wood, and the sound of
outer ocean on a beach.*
~~ Henry beston, American Author 1888 – 1968

*Fireflies merrily dance along a summer breeze,
Crickets softly play their tiny strings in song,
Bull frogs adding rhythm like a musician's beating drum,
Cicadas raise their voice and sing along with the throng,
Oh, how I love summer's sweet music of the night,
Singing me to sleep like a sweet lullaby.*
~~ Catherine Pittman © 2015

10/2/2015 - 10/4/2015
Everett Sausage Festival
Our Lady of Perpetual Help Grounds - Everett, WA
www.everettsausagefest.com   (425) 314-2037

Admission: Not Provided
Kid Friendly Event
Hours: Fri & Sat: Noon - 12am; Sun: Noon - 7pm

Vendor Contact: Alan Skranak esfvendors@gmail.com
# of Vendors: 50   Juried Event
Deadline: 8/1/15

Attendance: 25000
# of Years Held: 39

10/2/2015 - 11/1/2015
Georgetown Morgue
5000 E Marginal Way S - Seattle, WA
www.seattlehaunts.com   (206) 762-2067

Paid Admission
Kid Friendly Event

Vendor Contact: info@seattlehaunts.com

I am struck by the simplicity of light in the atmosphere in the autumn, as if the earth absorbed none, and out of this profusion of dazzling light came the autumnal tints.
~~ Henry David Thoreau, October 12, 1852

10/2/2015 - 10/3/2015
Inland Northwest Craft
Beer Festival
602 N Havana St. Spokane, WA
99202 - Spokane, WA
www.washingtonbeer.com
(206) 795-5510

The Inland Northwest Craft Beer Festival will welcome 30 craft breweries pouring more than 100 types of beer. To commemorate America's other favorite pastime, the event will be held at Avista Satdium and features live music, great food and baseball-themed fun.

Paid Admission
Kid Friendly Event
Hours: Friday, 4:00-8:00pm Saturday, Noon-8:00pm

# of Vendors: 30 breweries
Attendance: 2000

10/2/2015 - 10/3/2015
Leavenworth Oktoberfest
Bavarian Village - Leavenworth, WA
www.leavenworthoktoberfest.com (425) 445-6183

Admission: Not Provided
Kid Friendly Event

Vendor Contact: info@leavenworthoktoberfest.com
Deadline: 9/1/15

Attendance: 15000
# of Years Held: 19

...September days are here, with summer's best of weather, and autumn's best of cheer. ~~ Helen Hunt Jackson

10/2/2015 - 11/1/2015
Nightmare on I-9
9010 Marsh Rd - Snohomish , WA
www.seattlehaunts.com   (206) 762-2067

Paid Admission
Kid Friendly Event
Hours: See website schedule

Email Contact: info@seattlehaunts.com

10/2/2015 - 10/4/2015
Washington State Evergreen Fall RV Show
Evergreen State Fairgrounds - Monroe, WA
www.evergreenfallrvshow.com   (206) 248-8430

Largest RV Show between Seattle and the Canadian
Border

Paid Admission
Hours: Friday 10am to 7pm Saturday, 10am to 7pm
            Sunday, 10am to 5pm

Vendor Contact: Bill Bradley bbwestlake@seanet.com
# of Vendors: N/A
Attendance: 10000   # of Years Held: 34

10/3/2015 - 10/4/2015
16th Annual Birdfest & Bluegrass Celebration
Ridgefield Community Center & Davis Park - Ridgefield,
WA
www.ridgefieldfriends.org   (360) 887-2033

Admission: Not Provided

Vendor Contact: Lucy Krantz lucyk88720@gmail.com
Attendance: 4,000 - 5,000
# of Years Held: 16

10/3/2015 - 10/3/2015
Bus Barn Bonanza
Auburn School District Transportation Yard - Auburn, WA
www.busbarnbonanza.com

Admission: Not Provided
Hours: 9am - 4pm

Vendor Contact: Ginger gingerkkelley@comcast.net

10/3/2015 - 10/4/2015
Mobile Food Rodeo 2015
Marymoor Park - Redmond, WA
www.mobilefoodrodeo.com

Admission: Not Provided
No Kid's Activities

Vendor Contact: vendors@piranhablonde.com

10/3/2015 - 10/3/2015
Old Apple Tree Festival
Old Apple Tree Park - Vancouver, WA
(360) 487-8308

Free Admission   Kid Friendly Event

Vendor Contact: jessica.antoine@cityofvancouver.us

10/3/2015 - 10/4/2015
Packwood Fall Craft Fair
Packwood Community Center - Packwood, WA
(800) 366-8201

Admission: Not Provided
Hours: Sat: 10am - 5pm; Sun: 10am - 4pm

Vendor Contact: lynn Price
mlynnprice@centurytel.net
# of Vendors: 30   Attendance: 1000

10/3/2015 - 10/4/2015
Spokane Renaissance Faire
Back of the Bluff at Green Bluff - Spokane, WA
https://www.facebook.com/pages/The-Spokane-Renaissance-Faire/225544414141486
(509) 998-3943

Admission: Not Provided
Kid Friendly Event
Hours: Sat: 10am - 5pm; Sun: 10am - 5pm

# of Vendors: 35

Attendance: 3000
# of Years Held: 5

10/6/2015 - 10/10/2015
Holiday Harvest Craft Show
Local 302 Union Hall - Bothell, WA
www.starvinghousewives.com   (206) 920-2957

Admission: Not Provided
No Kid's Activities
Hours: Tues - Fri: 10am-8pm; Sat: 10am-6pm

# of Vendors: 70   Juried Event
Deadline: 9/1/15

Attendance: 2000

10/8/2015 - 10/8/2015
Witches Night Out
Country Village Shops - Bothell, WA
www.countryvillagebothell.com

Halloween season begins with the annua Witches Night Out! So come in your best sppoky witches outfit for some fun!

Free Admission   Kid Friendly Event
Hours: 6pm - 8pm

10/9/2015 - 11/15/2015
Celebration of Western and Wildlife Art Show
Puyallup Fair Grounds - Expo Hall - Puallup, WA
www.fredoldfieldcenter.org   253-752-9616

Quick Draws, Live Auctions, Over 100 of the country's top Western & Wildlife Artists & Country Music.   With something for everyone, it's the perfect Family venue! There's excitement in the air as artists gather from the Western half of the United States to bring you this show. It brings together a diverse array of talent and hard to fathom where else you can feast your eyes on a display- -- all under one roof. Spend your day wandering through art displays, Enjoy meeting artists and watching art demonstrations.   Designed to engage students of all ages in a guided, creative learning experience.

Free Admission & Parking
Kid Friendly Event
Hours: Fri 3-10pm   Sat 10am-10pm   Sun 10am - 5pm

Vendor Contact: Joella Oldfield Foldfield@comcast.net
# of Vendors: 100+   Juried Event

# of Years Held: 25

10/9/2015 - 10/11/2015
Dungeness Crab & Seafood Festival
Port Angeles City Pier - Port Angeles, WA
www.crabfestival.org   (360) 452-6300

Admission: Not Provided
Kid Friendly Event
Hours: Fri: 4pm - 8:30 pm;
         Sat: 11am - 8:30 pm; Sun: 11am - 5pm

Vendor Contact: operations@crabfestival.org
# of Vendors: 45   Juried Event
Deadline: 5/10/15   # of Years Held: 14

10/9/2015 - 10/11/2015
Oktoberfest Northwest
Washington State Fair Events Center - Puyallup, WA
www.oktoberfestnw.com   (425) 295-3262

The 3-day festival includes a Munich-inspired Festhalle Biergarten, authentic entertainment, traditional German foods, a Stein Dash 5K, the Hammerschlagen Tournament of Champions, Wiener Dog races, pumpkin decorating, and fun games for all ages.

Paid Admission
Kid Friendly Event

Hours: (subject to change) - Friday- Noon - midnight
            Saturday - 11a - midnight
            Sunday - 11a - 6pm

NOTE: Families are welcome in the Festhalle Biergarten until 7 p.m. each evening (Sunday, families are welcome all day!); for the remainder of the evening, guests must be 21 years of age or older.

Vendor Contact: Festivals Inc. info@festivals-inc.com
# of Years Held: 11

10/10/2015 - 10/11/2015
Cranberry Harvest Festival
Community Hall - Grayland, WA
www.westportgrayland-chamber.org
(360) 267-6107

Admission: Not Provided
Hours: Sat: 10am-6pm; Sun: 10am-3pm

# of Vendors: 5
Attendance: 4000
# of Years Held: 19

Oktoberfest

NORTHWEST

Live Music and Dance
Washington's Largest
Oktoberfest-Themed Biergarten
Wiener Dog Races (Sun)
German Beer & Food
Free Kids' Activities / 5k Stein Dash
HAMMERSCHLAGEN

OCT 9-11, 2015
Washington State Fair Events Center
Puyallup, WA - WE'RE INDOORS

10/10/2015 - 10/10/2015
Mason/Benson Craft Bazaar
5971 E. Mason Lake Dr. West - Grapeview, WA
www.mbcwa.com   (360) 427-3559

Come to THE MBC HOLIDAY CRAFT BAZAAR!!! This
event is held at the Mason/Benson Lake Community
Center Join us for a unique shopping experience. Local
artists and crafters are selling their wares just in time for
some early holiday shopping. We're even serving a hot
4-7300Enter our raffle to win a beautiful gift basket!

Free Admission
No Kid's Activities
Hours: Saturday 9:00 am - 3:00 pm

Vendor Contact: Jan Means janpan55@live.com
# of Vendors: 32   Not a Juried Event
Deadline: 9/15/15

# of Years Held: 10

10/10/2015 - 10/10/2015
Mid-Columbia Duck Race
Columbia Park - Kennewick, WA
www.tcduckrace.com

Prizes, Vendors and lots of fun as the rubber duckies
race along to win the prize at this annual fundraiser.

Paid Admission
Kid Friendly Event

Vendor Contact: Katherine Vosahlo
katherine.vosahlo@scouting.org
Deadline: 6/1/15

10/10/2015 - 10/11/2015
Orting Pumpkin Fest
Orting Park - Orting, WA
www.tacomaevents.com   (253) 230-6851

Admission: Not Provided   Kid Friendly Event
Hours: 10am - 6pm

Vendor Contact: Gary Grape gwgrape47@comcast.net
# of Vendors: 50
Attendance: 3000   # of Years Held: 8

10/10/2015 - 10/10/2015
Puyallup Girls Night Out
South Hill Mall - Puyallup, WA
www.southhillmall.com   (253) 840-2828

Guests will enjoy a fabulous array of pampering,
shopping, entertainment, great food, prizes and fun!

Admission: Not Provided
No Kid's Activities

10/10/2015 - 10/10/2015
Renton Fall Harvest Festival
Piazza Park; Downtown Renton; So. 3rd & Burnett St
Renton, WA
www.piazzarenton.com   (206) 999-1733

14th annual Fall Harvest Festival. Arts and crafts,
music, food and entertainment. A community
celebration of the season including face painting,
pumpkin decorating, zombies and more! Come join us
for a fun and festive day!

Free Admission   Kid Friendly Event
Hours: Saturday, 11:00 am - 4:00 pm

Vendor Contact: Cheryl Scheuerman
info@piazzarenton.com
# of Vendors: 60   Not a Juried Event
Deadline: 9/25/15   # of Years Held: 14

10/11/2015
Seattle Children's Festival
Seattle Center Grounds - Seattle, WA
www.nwfolklife.org   (206) 684-7300

A one-day multi-cultural festival. The festival brings
together local communities to celebrate families in the
Northwest. Featuring performances and interactive
workshops specifically geared towards families with
children of all ages.

Free Admission
Kid-Friendly Event

Attendance: 3,000+
# of Years: 2

10/16/2015 - 10/16/2015
Wenatchee Fall Arts & Crafts Show
Town Toyota Center - Wenatchee, WA
www.custershows.com   (509) 924-0588

Admission: Not Provided
Hours: Fri: 10am-8pm;
           Sat: 10am-6pm; Sun: 10am-4pm

Vendor Contact: info@custersshows.com
# of Vendors: 100   Juried Event

# of Years Held: 3

It is no longer good enough to cry peace. We must act peace,
live peace and live in peace.
American Indian Proverb – Shenandoah Tribe

10/22/2015 - 10/25/2015
Tacoma Holiday Food & Gift Festival
Tacoma Dome - Tacoma, WA
www.HolidayGiftShows.com
(800) 521-7469

You'll find arts and crafts, gifts, gourmet foods, holiday décor and entertainment all under the Tacoma Dome. Come visit with artists in the Artists in Action area, bring the little ones down for a visit with Santa, learn culinary secrets from local chefs in the Cooking for the Holidays section and enjoy festive entertainment by local schools and studios. Pay once and return for free all 4 days.

Paid Admission
Kid Friendly Event
Hours: Th-Fr 10am-9pm Sat 10am-8pm Sun 10am-6pm

Vendor Contact: Susie O'Brien Borer - Show Manager
Tacoma@ShowcaseEvents.org
# of Vendors: 500   Juried Event
Deadline: 10/1/15
Attendance: 40000   # of Years Held: 33

10/23/2015 - 10/24/2015
Autumn Arts & Crafts Festival
WSU Beasley Coliseum - Pullman, WA
www.palouse.net/dlgenterprises/index.html
(509) 332-5206

Admission: Not Provided
Hours: Fri: 10am-8pm; Sat: 9am-5pm

Vendor Contact: Don Gallagher
dlgenterprises@turbonet.com
# of Vendors: 125   Juried Event
Deadline: 9/15/15

Attendance: 2500   # of Years Held: 7

10/24/2015 - 10/24/2015
Bell Ringer Bazaar
Vancouver Heights United Methodist Church
5701 McCarthur Blvd - Vancouver, WA
(360) 693-4761

Helps support the UMW Women's group.

Admission: Not Provided
Hours: 9am - 4pm

Vendor Contact: vancouverheightsumc@gmail.com

10/24/2015 - 10/24/2015
Halloween Harvest Festival
Washington Elementary School - Auburn, WA
www.auburnwa.gov   (253) 931-3043
Bring canned and boxed food to support the Auburn
Food Bank.

Free Admission   Kid Friendly Event
Hours: 2pm - 5pm

10/25/2015 - 10/25/2015
**Crush Me, Squeeze Me, Make Me Wine at the
Beach Festival**
Westport Winery - Westport, WA
www.westportwinery.org   (360) 648-2224

Your family will have a grape stomping good time at this
lively event. Live music, grape stomping, food and wine
tasting, Lucy & Ethyl look-alike contest and more!

Admission: Not Provided
Kid Friendly Event

10/31/2015 - 10/31/2015
Lighthouse Haunted Halloween
Grays Harbor Lighthouse - 1020 W Ocean Ave
Westport, WA
www.westportmaritimemusem.com
(360) 268-0078

A family-friendly haunted night at the Grays Harbor
Lighthouse!

Admission: Not Provided
Kid Friendly Event

10/31/2015 - 10/31/2015
Safe Halloween
Country Village Shops - Bothell, WA
www.countryvillagebothell.com

Come all ye ghost, goblins and ghouls for a safe
Halloween celebration! Come in costume and trick-or-
treat throught the shops.

Free Admission
Kid Friendly Event
Hours: 4pm - 6pm

*Black & White
Leaves
© Zdenet
All Free
Downloads*

November 2015

11/5/2015 - 11/5/15 (Tentative)
Crystal Plum Bazaar
Alki Middle School - Vancouver, WA

Admission: Not Provided
Hours: 9-4pm

Vendor Contact: Vancouver Dawn Lions Club
# of Vendors: 100

11/5/2015 - 11/7/2015
Pickering Barn Christmas Craft Show
Pickering Barn - Issaquah, WA
www.countrycreation.blogspot.com
(425) 413-1004

Free Admission

Vendor Contact: Sandy Roundy
srroundy@comcast.net
# of Vendors: 65   Juried Event

11/6/2015 - 11/8/2015
Children's Hospital Craft Show
Ocasta Recreational Hall - Ocosta, WA
(360) 268-9003

This arts and crafts bazaar benefits the Children's Hospital in Seattle. Enjoy shopping the handmade wares and support the Children's Hospital!

Admission: Not Provided

11/6/2015 - 11/7/2015
Home Made for the Holidays Bazaar
Thurston Expo Center Heritage Hall - Olympia, WA
www.co.thurston.wa.us   (360) 491-0176

Admission: Not Provided
Vendor Contact: Debbie Wakefield   Juried Event

11/6/2015 - 11/7/2015
Kent Holiday Craft Market
Kent Senior Activity Center - Kent, WA
www.kentholidaycraftmarket.com (253) 856-5150

Featuring the famous Figgy Pudding Café and Bake Sale, plus 70 vendor booths of handcrafted one-of-a-kind gifts... all in one place! Door price drawings and live holiday music too!

Admission: Not Provided

Vendor Contact: Cindy Robinson
crobinson@kentwa.gov
# of Vendors: 70   Juried Event

Attendance: 2200   # of Years Held: 29

Halloween Still Life ©
Jeanette O'Neal
All Free Downloads

11/6/2015 - 11/8/2015
Pasco Christmas Arts & Crafts Show
TRAC Center - Pasco, WA
www.custershows.com   (509) 924-0588

Gourmet foods, handmade wares and a festive holiday atmosphere makes for a unique arts and crafts show. From whimsical bird house to blown glass vases, handpainted potery to huckleberry products and much, much more! Free samples too!

Admission: Not Provided
Hours: Fri 10am-9pm; Sat 9am-7pm; Sun 10am-5pm

Vendor Contact: info@custershows.com
# of Vendors: 150   Juried Event

Attendance: 11000
# of Years Held: 20

11/7/2015 - 11/7/2015
26th Annual A Note-able Affair Craft Fair
Burlington Edison High School
301 N Burlington Blvd - Burlington, WA

Experience a touch of Europe at this annual holiday market! Reminiscent of the old world, European Christmas markets. You will be delighted at the sights and sounds of the season in this charming village atmosphere.

Free Admission
Hours: 8:30 am - 4pm

Vendor Contact: becraftfair@hotmail.com

11/7/2015 - 11/7/2015
BabyFest
Seattle Center - Seattle, WA
www.babyfestnw.com   (360) 514-0767

The Northwest's Biggest Baby Shower!

Paid Admission   Kid Friendly Event
Hours: VIP Entry 10am;
        Show Hours: 11am-4pm

Vendor Contact: Lori lori@pintsizedproductions.com

11/7/2015 - 11/9/2015
Cultural Crossroads Festival
Crossroads Stage & South Concourse - Bellevue, WA
www.crossroadsbellevue.com/SpecialEvents/Cultu
ralCrossroadsFestival   (206) 443-1410

Admission: Not Provided
Hours: Sat: 10am-10pm; Sun: 11am-6pm

Vendor Contact: ehc@seattle.gov

11/7/2015 - 11/8/2015
Great Train Expo
Washington State Fair Events Center - Puyallup, WA
www.greattrainexpo.com   (630) 608-4988

Paid Admission
Kid Friendly Event

Email Contact: bill@trainexpoinc.com

Leaves dancing in the wind and the air filled with the scent of crisp and golden apples. There's a sense of anticipation as nature performs her last glorious array of colorful art. ~~ Catherine Pittman © 2015

11/7/2015 - 11/8/2015
Ladies Auxillary Fall Bazaar
Wild West VFM Post 91 - Tacoma, WA
(253) 883-1975

Admission: Not Provided
Hours: 9am - 4pm

# of Years Held: 3

11/7/2015 - 11/7/2015
Mountlake Terrace High Holiday Bazaar
Mountlake Terrace High School - 21801 44th Ave
Mountlake Terrace, WA

Free Admission
Hours: 9am - 4pm

Vendor Contact: mthsbazaar@gmail.com

11/7/2015 - 11/8/2015
North Kitsap Holiday Fest
North Kitsap High School - Poulsbo, WA
www.nkschools.org/page/6590   (360) 598-8420

Admission: Not Provided
Hours: Sat: 930am - 6pm; Sun: 11am - 4pm

# of Vendors: 112   Juried Event
Attendance: 2000

From ghoulies and ghosties and long-leggedy beasties,
And things that go bump in the night,
Good Lord, deliver us!
~~ Scottish Saying

October, the extravagant sister, has ordered an immense
amount of the most gorgeous forest tapestry for her grand
reception.
~~Oliver Wendell Holmes, Poet 1809-1894

11/7/2015 - 11/7/2015
Seattle Women's Life Style Expo
Washington State Fair Grounds Expo Hall - Seattle, WA
www.womensdayoutexpo.com   (602) 625-3000

An event for women to come together, bond, be educated, be inspired and uplifed while enjoying the things women love to do! Designed for women of all ages. Spend the day exploring fashion, beauty, lifestyle or health, this expo brings together these resources in one place.

Admission: Not Provided
No Kid's Activities

Vendor Contact: info@womensdayoutexpo.com
Deadline: 9/23/15

11/7/2015 - 11/8/2015
University High School Fall Craft Fair
University High School - Spokane Valley, WA
www.uhicraftfairspokanevalley.weebly.com/detail
s.html
(509) 995-5340

Proceeds go tward the highschool's music program and its students! Featuring holiday decorations, home décor, jellies and james, jewery and more.

Admission: Not Provided
Hours: Sat: 9am-5pm; Sun: 10am - 4pm

Vendor Contact: Tracy Ferguson
uhicraftfair@gmail.com
# of Vendors: 140

Attendance: 2500

11/7/2015 - 11/7/2015
Woodinville Holiday Craft Fair
Woodmoor Elementary School - Bothell, WA
www.statefairpark.org/p/central-wa-state-fair

Lots of excellent shopping form artisans and their handcrafted wares! There is somethine new every year, so come join us for this great event.

Admission: Not Provided
Hours: 9am - 5pm

Vendor Contact:
sepacwoodinvillecraftfair@gmail.com
# of Vendors: 85   # of Years Held: 35

11/7/2015 - 11/7/2015
Woodinville Women's Show
The Y at the Carol Edwards Center, 17401 133rd Ave NE, Woodinville - Woodinville, WA
www.WoodinvilleWomensShow.com   425-483-0606

The 8th Annual Woodinville Women's Show is back with FREE admission and another great mix of vendors! More than 50 local, women-owned and women-focused businesses will display an array of products and services targeted specifically toward women. Exhibitors will have interactive demonstrations and presentations on topics ranging from healthcare and wellness, to business opportunities and fashion. Children Welcome. FREE Coffee Bar.

Free Admission
No Kid's Activities
Hours: Saturday 10am-2pm

Vendor Contact: Julie Boselly julie@woodinville.com
# of Vendors: 55   Not a Juried Event
Deadline: 9/30/15
Attendance: 250   # of Years Held: 8

11/10/2015 - 11/14/2015
Echo Falls Holiday Home & Gift Show
Echo Falls Country Club - Snohomish, WA
www.starvinghousewives.com   (206) 920-2957

Featuring handmade wares for your gift-giving or home!

Admission: Not Provided
Hours: Tues-Fri: 10am-8pm; Sat: 10am-6pm

# of Vendors: 70   Juried Event
Deadline: 9/1/15/15

Attendance: 2000

11/12/2015 - 11/14/2015
Port Orchard Chocolate Festival
Port Orchard Pavillion Event Center - Port Orchard, WA
www.fathomsoffun.org   (360) 710-3087

Admission: Not Provided
Hours: Fri: 6:30pm-10:30pm; Sat: 10am-6pm; Sun:
11am-5pm

Vendor Contact: Al Mahaney
              # of Years Held: 3

11/12/2015 - 11/14/2015
Vasa Park Christmas Craft Show
Vasa Park - Bellevue, WA
www.countrycreation.blogspot.com (425) 413-1004

Free Admission

Vendor Contact: Sandy Roundy
srroundy@comcast.net
# of Vendors: 95   Juried Event

11/12/2015 - 11/12/15 (tentative)
Washougal High School Holiday Marketplace
Washougal High School - 1201 39th St - Washougal, WA
www.washougal.k12.wa.us/WHS/athletics_activiti
es/bazaar.htm

Admission: Not Provided

Vendor Contact: whsinfo@washougal.k12.wa.us

11/13/2015 - 11/15/2015
2015 Northwest Fall Art & Fine Craft Show
Hangar 30 at Warren G Magnuson park - Seattle, WA
www.nwartalliance.com   (206) 525-5926

Amazing handcrafted works for your holiday shopping
and decorating! Free children's art table for the kids!

Admission: Not Provided
Kid Friendly Event
Hours: Fri & Sat: 10am - 6pm; Sun: 10am - 5pm

Vendor Contact: info@nwartalliance.com
# of Vendors: 110   Juried Event
Deadline: 5/31/15

11/13/2015 - 11/15/2015
Fine Art & Holiday Gifts at Fauntleroy
Fauntleroy Church - Seattle, WA
www.fauntleroyucc.org   (206) 932-5600

Free Admission
Hours: Fri: 5pm - 8pm;
          Sat: 10am - 4pm; Sun: 11am - 2pm

Juried Event

---

*I entreat all artisans faithfully to follow their craft and take
delight in it.*
~~ Jan Hus, Cezechoslovakian Philosopher 1369 - 1415

11/13/2015 - 11/15/2015
Puyallup Gem Faire
Washington State Fair Events Center - Puyallup, WA
www.gemfaire.com   (503) 252-8300

Fine jewelry, precious & semi-precious gemstones, millions of beads, crystals, gold & silver, minerals & much more at manufacturer's prices. Over 70 exhibitors from around the world. Jewelry repair & cleaning while you shop. Free hourly door prizes. For more info, visit www.gemfaire.com or call (503) 252-8300 or email: info@gemfaire.com.

Paid Admission   No Kid's Activities
Hours: Fri Noon-6pm,
          Sat 10am-6pm, Sun 10am-5pm

Vendor Contact: Allen Van Volkinburgh
info@gemfaire.com
# of Vendors: 70   Not a Juried Event
Deadline: Until Full

Attendance: 3000
# of Years Held: 26

11/14/2015 - 11/14/2015
Christmas in Telemark
Issaquah Senior Center & Veteran's Memorial Field -
Issaquah, WA
www.scandianavianfestivals.com   (425) 313-0193

Free Admission
Hours: 10am - 4pm

Vendor Contact: Leiann Ronnestad
info@barnefoundation.com
# of Vendors: 30

Attendance: 1000

11/14/2015 - 11/15/2015
Fall Folk Festival 2015
Spokane Community College - Spokane, WA
www.spokanefolkfestival.org   (509) 628-3663

Admission: Not Provided
Kid Friendly Event
Hours: Sat: 11-10; Sun: 11-5

Vendor Contact: fallfolkfestival@moxxee.com

Attendance: 7000
# of Years Held: 20

11/14/2015 - 11/14/2015
Mountain View High School Holiday Bazaar
Mountain View High School - 1500 SE Blairmont Dr -
Vancouver, WA
www.mvband.org/holiday-bazaar.htm l

Admission: Not Provided
Hours: 9am - 4pm

Vendor Contact: blue.thunder.band@gmail.com
# of Vendors: 150

11/14/2015 - 11/14/2015
Shorewood Holiday Bazaar
Shorewood Elementary School - Burien, WA
www.facebook.com/pages/Shorewood-PTA-
Holiday-Bazaar/269691019731130

Admission: Not Provided

Vendor Contact: Cecilia Schukar
coachcecilia@comcast.net
# of Vendors: 60

11/14/2015 - 11/14/2015
Southridge Music Booster's Holiday Bazaar
Southridge High School - 3520 Southridge Blvd
Kennewick, WA
www.southridgemusic.com/holiday-bazaar.html

Paid Admission (children under 12 are free)
Hours: 9am - 4pm

Vendor Contact: Shsmusicboosters@veachco.net

11/14/2015 - 11/15/2015
St. Brendan School Holiday Craft Fair
St. Brendan School - Bothell, WA
www.school.saintbrendan.org/programs/craft_fai
r.php   (425) 483-8300

Free Admission
Hours: Sat: 9am - 5pm; Sun: noon - 4pm

Vendor Contact: saintbrendancraftfair@gmail.com
# of Vendors: 100
Juried Event
Deadline: 6/10/15

Attendance: 5000

11/20/2015 - 11/21/2015
Funky Junk Sisters: Junk Salvation
Washington State Fairgrounds - Puyallup, WA
www.funkyjunksisters.com

Admission: Not Provided

Vendor Contact: funkyjunksisters@live.com

11/20/2015 - 11/20/2015
Spokane Christmas Arts & Crafts Show
Spokane Fair & Expo Center - Spokane, WA
www.custershows.com   (509) 924-0588

Admission: Not Provided

Vendor Contact: info@custershows.com
# of Vendors: 300   Juried Event

Attendance: 15000
# of Years Held: 39

11/21/2015 - 11/21/2015
2015 Holiday Bazaar
Greywolf School - 171 Carlsborg Rd - Sequim, WA
www.greywolfpta.com   (360) 582-3300

Admission: Not Provided

Vendor Contact: Greywolfholidaybazaar@gmail.com

11/21/2015 - 11/21/2015
2015 My Friends & More Holiday Bazaar
International Union of Operating Engineers hall
18701 120th Ave NE - Bothell, WA
www.craftybug.com

Free Admission
Hours: 10am - 5pm

Vendor Contact: bazaarinfo@craftybug.com

As we express our gratitude, we must never forget that the
highest appreciation is not to utter words, but to live by them.
~~John Fitzgerald Kennedy, US President 1917-1963

11/21/2015 - 11/22/2015
Hassle Free Holiday Bazaar
Renton Community Center - 1715 SE Maple Valley Hwy
Renton, WA
www.rentonwa.gov/HolidayBazaar/ (425) 430-6700

This event attracts visitors and vendors from the Puget
Sound area.

Admission: Not Provided
Kid Friendly Event
Hours: Fri: 11am - 6pm; Sat: 9am - 5pm

# of Vendors: 100
Juried Event

11/21/2015 - 11/21/2015
HUGE PRE-BLACK FRIDAY HOLIDAY BAZAAR
Renton Technical College, 3000 NE 4th St - Renton, WA
(206) 679-7441

HUGE PRE-BLACK FRIDAY HOLIDAY BAZAAR Get a jump
start on your holiday shopping! Bring family and friends
for a fun-filled day of food, free door prizes, raffles, and
quality vendors "many with special pricing just for this
event!"   Toys, jewelry, handmade crafts, artwork, skin
care, soaps, purses, cards, children's™ items, books,
digital solutions, home décor, hair accessories, candles,
dolls, and so much more!

Free Admission
Kid Friendly Event
Hours: 9am-4pm

Vendor Contact: holidaybazaar@live.com
# of Vendors: 50
Deadline: 10/15/15

Attendance: 600
# of Years Held: 6

11/21/2015 - 11/21/2015
Meeker Mansion Craft Show
Meeker Mansion 312 Spring St - Puyallup, WA
www.meekermansion.org   (253) 848-1770

Holiday decorations and unique handcrafted gifts for sale
at this historic Victorian mansion.

Admission: Not Provided
Hours: 10am - 5pm

11/21/2015 - 11/22/2015
12/5/2015 – 12/6/2015
North Vancouver Holiday Bazaar
Carson Graham Secondary School, 2145 Jones Ave
North Vancouver, Canada
www.nvholidaybazaar.com

Join us for our 2nd Annual North Vancouver Holiday
Bazaar, happening November 21-22, and December 5-6
at Carson Graham Secondary School! With over 100
vendors a day, each day has new vendors showcasing
their handmade products from right here in BC! $2
admission and the first 150 guests - and kids 12 and
under - get in free. Gather your friends, mark your
calendar, and plan on joining us for this popular and
festive Bazaar!

Paid Admission
Kid Friendly Event
Hours: Two Weekends 10am-4pm each day.

Vendor Contact: Caterina Reid or Chris Kennedy
nvholidaybazaar@gmail.com
# of Vendors: 100+   Juried Event
Deadline: 1st round: August 15 2015

Attendance: 1000+ per day
# of Years Held: 2

11/21/2015 - 11/22/2015
Northwest Woodcarvers Show & Sale
Western Washington Fairgrounds - Puyallup, WA
www.woodcarvers.org   (360) 273-0977

Admission: Not Provided
Hours: Sat: 10am - 5pm; Sun: 10am - 4pm

Vendor Contact: John Templar
stringwalker420@msn.com
# of Vendors: 30   Juried Event

Attendance: 2000
# of Years Held: 35

11/21/2015 - 11/22/2015
NWCA 35th Annual "Artistry in Wood" Show & Sale
330 S. Meridian at the Pioneer Park Pavillion
PUYALLUP, WA
www.woodcarvers.org
(253) 732-6957 or (253) 833-4626

Northwest Carvers Association Juried Show & Sale Joe
McConnell, featured artist   Show Features: Juried
Carving Gallery, Ribbons & Cash Awards, Free Demos
each day, Raffles, Auction, Spec. Awards, Seminars,
Carving Sales, Tools, Books & Wood sales. Wheel Chair
Accessible, Free Parking.

Contact dthompson695@life.com   or
c.l.harkness@q.com   or www.woodcarvers.org for
more information. $7 ticket is good for 2 days. Children
12 and under free.

Paid Admission
No Kid's Activities
Hours: Saturday 10am to 5pm Sunday 10am to 4pm

Juried Event   # of Years Held: 35 years

NWESC • PO Box 1324 • Monroe, WA 98272
www.NWESC.org • info@NWESC.org
(206) 940-8589

Monroe, WA

www.nwesc.org

11/21/2015 - 11/21/2015
NWESC's 5th Annual Holiday
Bazaar

17922 149th St SE
(First Baptist Church)

(360) 794-0870

Northwest Equine Stewardship Center is having their 5th Annual Holiday Bazaar on Sat., Nov. 21 in Monroe, WA. Come have a fun day that includes holiday shopping, delicious bake sale, hot lunch, silent auction, raffles of vendors' items, Kids' Corner, photos with Santa Pony, and more! Northwest Equine Stewardship Center (NWESC) is a non-profit organization dedicated to providing professional level rehabilitative care (veterinary, hoof care, training) to rescue horses.

Free Admission
Kid Friendly Event
Hours: Saturday, November 21, 10am - 4pm

Vendor Contact: Crystal Apple bazaar@nwesc.org
# of Vendors: 80+   Not a Juried Event
Deadline: Until Full

# of Years Held: 5

For flowers that bloom about our feet;
For tender grass, so fresh, so sweet;
For song of bird, and hum of bee;
For all things fair we hear or see,
Father in heaven, we thank Thee!
~~Ralph Waldo Emerson, Poet 1803 - 1882

11/21/2015 - 11/21/2015
Olympia High School Bearzaar
1302 North Street
(Olympia High School) - Olympia, WA
www.olympia.osd.wednet.edu/information/bearza
ar   (360) 956-3667

Over 160 antique & handcrafted vendors. Chance the raffle & visit with friends over lunch or lattes. Always the Saturday before Thanksgiving.

Admission: Suggested Donation
Kid Friendly Event
Hours: Sat 9am-4pm

Vendor Contact: Kathy Thompson
remax@kathythompson.net
# of Vendors: 170   Juried Event

Attendance: 3000
# of Years Held: 15

11/21/2015 - 11/21/2015
Silver Bells 4th Christmas Bazaar
The Apex - Camas, WA
www.facebook.com/Silver.Bells.Christmas.Bazaar

You'll find plenty of special treasures!   Unopened pet food and blankets for donation is appreciated!

Admission: Not Provided

Vendor Contact: Larina Boyd
# of Vendors: 60

Attendance: 500
# of Years Held: 4

11/27/2015 - 11/28/2015
Festive Shopping Experience Bazaar
Thurston County Fairgrounds - Lacey, WA
(360) 491-0176

Come experience this festive shopping event! Handcrafted holiday treasures and gourmet treats, children's area and more. Accepts donations of non-perishable food items for the Thurston County Food Bank.

Free Admission
Hours: Fri: 12pm-5pm; Sat: 9am-5pm

# of Vendors: 100

11/27/2015 - 11/28/2015
Holiday Craft Sale 2015
Port Townsend Community Center - Port Townsend, WA
www.porttownsendartsguild.org   (360) 774-6544

Free Admission
Hours: 10am - 5pm

Vendor Contact: Donna Harding & Jess Hogan
ptartsguild@yahoo.com

Juried Event
Attendance: 5000

11/27/2015 - 11/28/2015
Lacey Holiday Bazaar
Fairgrounds - Lacey, WA
www.co.thurston.wa.us   (360) 786-5453

Free Admission
Hours: Fri: noon - 5; Sat: 9am - 5pm

Vendor Contact: bodnark@co.thurston.wa.us
# of Vendors: 100   Juried Event

11/27/2015 - 12/24/2015
Snowflake Lane
Between Bellevue Square, Lincoln Square & Belevue Pl
Bellevue, WA

Free Admission
Kid Friendly Event
Hours: 7pm nightly

11/27/2015 - 11/29/2015
Winter Fanta-Sea Craft Show
Ocean Shores Convention Center - Ocean Shores, WA
www.oceanshoresinfo.com/osevents.html
360-289-9586

Free Admission
# of Vendors: 70

11/28/2015 - 1/2/2016
Garden d'Lights
Bellevue Botanical Gardens1
2001 Main St - Bellevue, WA
www.gardendlights.org   (425) 452-2750

Paid Admission   Kid Friendly Event

Vendor Contact: info@gardendlights.org

11/28/2015 - 11/29/2015
Holidays at the Beach
Downtown Long Beach - Long Beach, WA
www.holidayslongbeach.com   (360) 355-5085

Free Admission

Vendor Contact: Holly Beller

11/28/2015 - 12/13/2015
Homemade for the Holidays
Thurston County Fairgrounds - Lacey, WA

Admission: Not Provided
Hours: Every Fri & Saturday; 11am - 5pm

11/28/2015 - 11/29/2015
Winterfest Arts & Crafts Fair
Peninsula High School - Gig Harbor, WA
https://sites.google.com/a/edtools.psd401.net/w
interfest/   (253) 858-8674

Peninsula High is transformed into a winter wonderland filled with gourmet foods and handcrafted items. Student groups support the event by selling food to benefit their individual clubs.   Includes the Hall of Wreaths Silent Auction, food fair and holiday music performed by students highlight this annual event.

Free Admission
Hours: Sat: 9-5; Sun: 11-4

Vendor Contact: phswinterfest@gmail.com
# of Vendors: 200

Attendance: 4000
# of Years Held: 23

There is one day that is ours. There is one day when all we Americans who are not self-made go back to the old home to eat saleratus biscuits and marvel how much nearer to the porch the old pump looks than it used to. Thanksgiving Day is the one day that is purely American.
~~O. Henry, American Writer 1862 - 1910

December 2015

12/1/2015 - 12/23/2015
Issaquah Reindeer Festival
19525 SE 54th St - Issaquah, WA
www.cougarmountainzoo.org   (425) 391-5508

Take part in one of the most unique holiday events in
the Northwest!

Paid Admission
Hours: 10:30 am - 4:30 pm

12/2/2015 - 12/6/2015
A Victorian Country Christmas Festival
Puyallup Fair & Events Center - Puyallup, WA
www.avictoriancountrychristmas.com
(253) 770-0777

Step back in time and enjoy a victorian village filled with
handmade ornaments, decorations, fragrances, toys and
hundres of other gift ideas for everyone on your list!

Admission: Not Provided

Vendor Contact: avcchristmas@comcast.net
# of Vendors: 530   Juried Event
Attendance: 50000   # of Years Held: 28

12/2/2015 - 12/5/2015
Bellevue Hilltop Holiday Craft Show
Northwest Arts Center - Bellevue, WA
www.bellevuehilltopholidaycraftshow.com
(360) 668-1987

Free Admission
Hours: Wed - Fri: 10am-8pm;Sat: 10am-5pm

Vendor Contact: Cameron Amann
hilltop.crafts@frontier.com   Deadline: 11/15/15
# of Vendors: 80   # of Years Held: 17

12/4/2015 - 12/5/2015
Kent Commons Holiday Bazaar
Kent Commons - 525 4th Ave N - Kent, WA
www.kentwa.gov/KentCommonsHolidayBazaar/
(253) 856-5000,

Free Admission

Vendor Contact: cjordan@kentwa.gov
# of Vendors: 100
Deadline: 9/4/15

12/4/2015 - 12/5/2015
Lighted Boat Parade
Columbia River - Kennewick, WA
www.lightedboatparade.com   (509) 734-9599

Parade begins each night at 6pm under the Cable Bridge at Clover Island. Travels upriver on the Kenewick side along Colubia Park, then turns around to travel down the river at around 7:30 pm. An additional loop for everyone on Clover Island is made before heading back to the Clover Island Marina at approximately 9pm.

Free Admission   Kid Friendly Event
Hours: 6pm - 9pm

Vendor Contact: Larry Kuga ci.yachtclub@gmail.com

Christmas Decorations
© George Hodan
All Free Downloads

12/4/2015 - 12/4/2015
Wintertide Celebration
Downtown Everett at the Plaza - Everett, WA
www.everettwa.gov/765/Festivals-Events
(425) 257-7117

Annual tree lighting with Santa and the Mayor, giant gingerbread house decoration, arts & crafts, children's activities, hot cider, cocoa and cookies by the bonfire, caroling, choral performances, holiday photo booth, stuff-a-truck with toys, hats, gloves and scarves for the local needy and more!

Free Admission
Kid Friendly Event

Vendor Contact: Lisa Newland
lnewland@everettwa.gov

12/5/2015 - 12/6/2015
2nd Annual North Vancouver Holiday Bazaar
Carson Graham Secondary School - 2145 Jones Ave
Vancouver, WA
www.nvholidaybazaar.com/

Admission: Not Provided

Vendor Contact: nvholidaybazaar@gmail.com

Photo by Public Domain Pictures
All Free Downloads

12/5/2015 - 12/5/2015
Auburn Winter Bus Barn Bonanza
Auburn School District Transportation Yard - Auburn, WA
www.busbarnbonanza.com

Free Admission
Hours: 9am- 4pm

Vendor Contact: Ginger gingerkkelley@comcast.net
Juried Event

12/5/2015 - 12/5/2015
Badger Mountain School Holiday Bazaar
Badger Mtn Elementary - 1515 Elementary St
Richland, WA
www.rsd.edu/schools/badger/badger-bazaar/
(509) 967-6225

Paid Admission (kids under 12 Free)

Vendor Contact: linda.dunford@rsd.edu

12/5/2015 - 12/5/2015
Hockinson Holdiday Bazaar
16819 NE 159th ST - Brush Prairie, WA
www.facebook.com/hockinsonhb   (360) 609-9389

The weather outside maybe frightful... But a Holiday
Bazaar is most delightful! Hockinson's Annual Holiday
Bazaar Crafters, Artists and Charitable Groups. Contact
hawkbazaar@outlook.com or 360 687-8117

Free Admission
Kid Friendly Event
Hours: 9am-4pm

Vendor Contact: Jenny Ristau
Hawkbazaar@outlook.com
# of Vendors: 82
Not a Juried Event   Deadline: 11/15/15# of Years
Held: 9

12/5/2015 - 12/5/2015
Kennedy Arts & Crafts Faire
John F Kennedy Catholic High School - Burien, WA

Student art show, area crafters booths, bake sale,
holiday music, raffles. All proceeds benefit the school.

Free Admission
Hours: 9am - 4pm

Vendor Contact: Gabby Jacobsen
# of Vendors: 140
Not a Juried Event   Deadline: 11/15/15
# of Years Held: 1500

12/5/2015 - 12/5/2015
Littlerock Elementary's 67th Annual Winterfest
Littlerock Elementary - 12710 Littlerock Rd SW
Olympia, WA

Enjoy this annual event.   Featuring a book fair,
Snowflake Café, cake walk, elf workshop, Santa, and
more! Proceeds help fund a college scholarship, student
enrichment programs and teacher allotment & requests.

Free Admission
Hours: 9am - 3pm

# of Vendors: 30+
# of Years Held: 67

Snow Bench
© *George Hodan*
All Free Downloads

12/5/2015 - 12/6/2015
North Vancouver Holiday Bazaar

Carson Graham Secondary School, 2145 Jones Avenue
North Vancouver, Canada
www.nvholidaybazaar.com

Join us for our 2nd Annual North Vancouver Holiday
Bazaar, happening November 21-22, and December 5-6
at Carson Graham Secondary School! With over 100
vendors a day, each day has new vendors showcasing
their handmade products from right here in BC! $2
admission and the first 150 guests - and kids 12 and
under - get in free. Gather your friends, mark your
calendar, and plan on joining us for this popular and
festive Bazaar!

Paid Admission
Kid Friendly Event
Hours: 10am-4pm each day.

Vendor Contact: Caterina Reid or Chris Kennedy
nvholidaybazaar@gmail.com
# of Vendors: 100+   Juried Event
Deadline: 1st round: August 15 2015

Attendance: 1000+ per day
# of Years Held: 2

12/5/2015 - 12/5/2015
Santa by the Sea

Westport Museum & Maritime Museum - Westport, WA
(253) 381-5989

Joyful children will love seeing Santa arrive at the
Westport Marina, and escort him to the Lens Building at
the Maritime Museum! Kids can have their photo taken
with Santa, play with pirates. Includes refreshments and
a special "kids only" store!

Admission: Not Provided   Kid Friendly Event

12/5/2015 - 12/5/2015
Seattle Christian School Christmas Bazaar
18301 Military Rd South - SeaTac, WA
(253) 946-9347

Free Admission
Hours: 9am - 4pm

Vendor Contact: Julie Norman jnorman20@juno.com

12/5/2015 - 12/5/2015
Spokane Community College Art/Craft/Food Fair
Spokane Community College - Spokane, WA
www.sites.scc.spokane.edu/ArtCraftFoodFair/

Admission: Not Provided
Vendor Contact: scccraftfair@gmail.com

12/5/2015 - 12/6/2015
TideFest Fine Arts & Crafts Celebration
Gig Harbor High - Gig Harbor, WA
www.tidefest.org   (253) 530-1478

Everything is handmade by the artist at this event!

Free Admission
Hours: Sat: 10am-5pm; Sun: 11am-4pm

Vendor Contact: Eleanor Ledbetter
eleanor@tidefest.org
# of Vendors: 150   Juried Event
Deadline: 5/1/15

Attendance: 6000
# of Years Held: 33

12/5/2015 - 12/5/2015
TYEE Holiday Bazaar
Highline Public Schools - 4424 S 188th St - SeaTac, WA
www.highlineschools.org   (206) 631-6430

Includes handmade & commercial items for sale, silent auction, pictures with Santa, kids' area, Christmas trees for sale and more!

Admission: Not Provided
Kid Friendly Event
Hours: 9am - 4pm

Vendor Contact: Alana Vinther
alana.vinther@highlineschools.org
# of Vendors: 100   Deadline: 10/1/15

12/5/2015 - 12/5/2015
University Place Winter Fest
Market Square in University Place (36th & Bridgeport Way W) - University Place, WA
www.cityofup.com/residents/events/university-place-winter-fest-december-5-2015
(253) 683-2992

Admission: Not Provided
Kid Friendly Event
Hours: 2pm - 6pm

Vendor Contact: Kimberly Halinen
Kimberly@VentiProductions.com

12/6/2015 - 12/6/2015
Edmonds Woodway High School Music Boosters Craft Fair
Edmonds Woodway High School - Edmonds, WA
www.facebook.com/pages/EdmondsWoodway-HS-Music-Boosters-Craft-Fair/1438008276479486

Free Admission

12/7/2015 - 12/7/2015
I'm Dreaming of a White Salmon Holiday Festival
Downtown - White Salmon, WA

The day begins with Santa's Breakfast and Bazaar from 7:30 - 11:30. Then at noon, the downtown shops will open with food, gift ideas, entertainment and more. From 2pm - 5pm the library sponsors hands-on crafts for kids, seasonal snacks and traditional wassail punch. From 4-6pm the outdoor fire pits will be lit for a fun feast, caroling, holiday boots, hot drinks and Santa. The grand finale at 5pm: Lighting of the Christmas tree!

Free Admission
Hours: 7:30am - 5pm

12/12/2015 - 12/13/2015
Chimacum Arts & Crafts Fair
Chimacum High School - Chimacum, WA

(360) 732-4015

Free Admission
Hours: 10am - 4pm

Vendor Contact: Flavia Heineman
Juried Event
Deadline: 6/30/15   # of Years Held: 29

Winter Landscapes ©
Larisa Koshkina
All Free Downloads

12/12/2015 - 12/13/2015
Port Gamble Country Chritmas
32159 NE Rainier Ave - Port Gamble, WA
www.portgamble.wix.com/countrychristmas
(360) 297-8074

Horse-drawn hayrides through the town that is sparkling with over 100,000 holiday lights, hands-on crafts for kids at Santa's workshop, the Northwest's oldest fruitcake contest, and much, much more!

Admission: Not Provided
Hours: Sat: 10am - 6pm; Sun: 11am - 3pm

12/19/2015 - 12/20/2015
Seattle Holiday Craft Fair
Warren G Magnuson Park Hangar 30 - Seattle, WA
www.renegadecraft.com   (773) 227-2707

Featuring a thoughtfully curated selection of the finest indie-craft goods, perfect for your holiday gift-giving and decorating needs.

Admission: Not Provided
Hours: 11am - 6pm

Vendor Contact: duggan@renegadecraft.com
Juried Event   Deadline: 9/25/15

...It came without ribbons! It came without tags! It came without packages, boxes or bags!... Then the Grinch thought of somethine he hadn't before! Maybe Christmas, he thought, doesn't come from a store. Maybe Christmas... perhaps... means a little bit more!
~~ Dr. Seuss (1904-1991), How the Grinch Stole Christmas!

January 2016

1/2/2016 - 1/3/2016
Tacoma Wedding Expo

Tacoma Dome Exhibition Hall - Tacoma, WA
www.bridesclub.com   (808) 768-5400

Admission: Not Provided
Hours: Sat: 10am-4pm; Sun: 11am-4pm

1/15/2016 - 1/24/2016
Winterfest
Lake Chelan, WA
www.lakechelan.com/winterfest

Paid Admission
Kid Friendly Event

Vendor Contact: Charles Sabian
csablan@cityofchelan.us

1/18/2016 - 1/18/2016
Martin Luther King Jr Birthday Celebration & March
Garfield High School - 23rd & East Jefferson St
Seattle, WA

Admission: Not Provided
Kid Friendly Event
Hours: Workshops: 9 - 9:50;
          Rallies: 10am - 11am;
          March: 12pm

1/27/2016 - 1/31/2016
Washington Sportsmen's Show
Washington State Fair Showplex Events Center
Puyallup, WA
www.otshows.com   (800) 343-6973

Paid Admission
Vendor Contact: info@otshows.com

1/28/2016 - 1/31/2016
Tacoma Home & Garden Show
Tacoma Dome - Tacoma, WA
www.otshows.com   (800) 343-6973

Paid Admission
Vendor Contact: info@otshows.com

1/30/2016 - 1/30/2016
Ground Frog Day
Downtown Snohomish - Snohomish, WA
www.groundfrogday.com

Come see our very own "Frognosticator Extraordinaire"
proclaim whether we will have an early or late spring!

Admission: Not Provided
Kid Friendly Event

# of Years Held: 11

The clock has struck midnight...
Another new year approaches so swiftly a new day draws near!
May this new year bring many joys to you,
And the Lord bless and keep you all year through.

It's one after midnight... a new year's begun!
With hope its wing and joy 'neath its sun.
What will we see in this baby new year,
I pray love and laughter will be near.
~~ Catherine Pittman © 1995 from the album
The Magic of Christmas

2/19/2016 - 2/21/2016
Washington State Horse Expo
Clark County Event Center - Ridgefield, WA
www.wastatehorseexpo.com   (360) 397-6170

Paid Admission

Vendor Contact: Heidi O'Hara
info@wastatehorseexpo.com

---

*It is the life of the crystal, the architect of the flake, the fire of
the frost, the soul of the sunbeam. This crisp winter air is full of
it. ~~ John Burroughs, American essayist 1837 – 1921
from "Winter Sunshine"*

*Kisses are a better fate than wisdom.
~~ E.E. Cummings, Poet 1894 – 1962*

*Grow old with me!
The best is yet to be.
~~ Robert Browning, Poet 1812 – 1889*

*Love looks not with the eyes, but with the mind,
And therefore is winged Cupid painted blind.
~~ William Shakespeare, Mid-Summer Night's Dream, 1595*

*Love is like a dew that falls on both nettles and lilies.
~~ Swedish Proverb*

March 2016

3/5/2016 - 3/5/2016
10th Annual Children's Festival
Westfield Vancouver Mall - Vancouver, WA
www.vancouverfamilymagazine.com
(360) 882-7762

Great family entertainment includes free face painting, balloon art, dance performances, samples, vendors, games and more!

Free Admission
Kid Friendly Event
Hours: 10am - 3pm

Vendor Contact: Nikki Klock
nikki@vancouverfamilymagazine.com

# of Years Held: 10

3/5/2016 - 3/5/16 (tentative)
Kent Kids' Art Day 2016
Kent Commons - Kent, WA
www.kentwa.gov/content.aspx?id=1434

Paid Admission
Kid Friendly Event
Hours: 10am - 4pm

Vendor Contact: Mark Hendrickson
mhendrickson@kentwa.gov Deadline: 1/7/16

Attendance: 500 - 600

3/12/2016 - 3/13/2016
Penn Cove Mussel Festival
Penn Cove & Downtown - Coupeville, WA
www.thepenncovemusselsfestival.com
(360) 678-5434

Admission: Not Provided
Hours: Fri: 5:30-8:30pm;
           Sat: 10am -9pm; Sun: 10am-5pm

3/2016 (TBA)
FrenchFest
Seattle Center Armory - Seattle, WA
www.fenpnw.org/portfolio/french-fest/
(206) 443-4703

Family-friendly event with live music, dance performances, French Fashion Show, international cuisine, game and other fun activities!

Admission: Not Provided
Kid Friendly Event

Vendor Contact: info@faccpnw.org

St. Patrick's Day is an enchanted time—a day to begin transforming winter's dreams into summer's magic.
~~Adrienne Cook

May your blessings outnumber the shamrocks that grow,
And may trouble avoid you wherever you go.
~~Irish Blessing

May your pockets be heavy and you heart be ligth,
May good luck pursue you each morning and each night.
~~Irish Blessing

April 2016

4/2/2016 - 4/2/2016
Beachcombers Driftwood Show
Westport Inn - Grayland, WA
www.westportwa.com/events/index.html
(360) 267-6532

Driftwood collectors exhibit their wares and compete.

Free Admission
Vendor Contact: Carolyn Barker

4/9/2016 - 4/10/16 (tentative)
International Children's Festival 2016
Seattle Center - Seattle, WA
www.childrensfest.tacawa.org

Paid Admission
Hours: 11am - 5:30 pm

4/9/2016 - 4/17/2016
The Daffodil Festival
Puyallup, WA
www.thedaffodilfestival.org   (253) 840-4194

The spirit of this diverse community shines at this Pierce County event! Featuring: Royalty Count Events, Daffodil Parade, Wekend festival, mutt show, Marine Parade, Junior Parde and more!

Admission: Not Provided
Kid Friendly Event
Hours: See event schedule online

4/14/2016 - 4/17/2016
Washington Spring Fair
Washington State Fair Events Center - Puyallup, WA
www.thefair.com

Contests, ducky derby, food, rides, animals, music & entertainment, kids fun zone, attractions, and more fun for the entire family!

Free Admission   Kid Friendly Event
Hours: See website in 2016

4/16/2016 - 4/17/2016
World Class Crab Races & Feed
Marina - Westport, WA
www.westportwa.com/events/index.html
(360) 268-9422

This thrilling event includes crab races & a feast of crab.

Paid Admission
Kid Friendly Event
Hours: Races: 1pm-3pm; Feast: 11am - 5pm

4/23/2016 - 4/24/16 (tentative)
Homespun Spring Bazaar 2016
Gary Weikel Event Center - Monroe, WA
(425) 319-2933

Admission: Not Provided
Hours: Sat: 10am-4pm; Sun: 10am-3pm

Vendor Contact: tmuchoney@comcast.net

Where man sees but withered leaves, God sees sweet flowers growing.
~~Albert Laighton, Poet 1829 - 1887

4/29/2016 - 5/1/2016
21st Annual Grays Harbor Shore Bird Festival
Hoquaim High School - Hoquaim, WA
www.shorebirdfestival.com   (800) 303-8498

Something for everyone can be found at this event! Marketplace with vendors and exhibitors, Saturday night dinner and speaker, nature fun fair with kids activities and more!

Admission: Not Provided
Kid Friendly Event

See the land, her Easter keeping,
Rises as her Maker rose.
Seeds, so long in darkness sleeping,
Burst at last from winter snows.
Earth with heaven above rejoices...
~~Charles Kingsley, Evangelical Priest and Novelist
1819 – 1875

Easter 2010 © Kevin Gardner

May 2016

5/1/2016 - 5/10/2016
Sequim Irrigation Festival & Street Fair
Downtown Sequim - Sequim, WA
www.irrigationfestival.com

Admission: Not Provided
Kid Friendly Event

# of Years Held: 121

5/6/2016 - 5/8/16 (tentative)
Packwood Mountain Festival
12990 US Hwy 12 - Packwood, WA
www.whitepasscountrymuseum.org/mountain_fes
tival.html

Admission: Not Provided
Kid Friendly Event

Vendor Contact: Martha Garoutte
magaroutte@centurytel.net

5/6/2016 - 5/8/2016
Washington Apple Blossom Fair 2016
Memorial Park - Wenatchee, WA
www.appleblossom.org

Admission: Not Provided

Vendor Contact: festival@appleblossom.org
Deadline: February 2016

Attendance: 100000
# of Years Held: 97

5/7/2016 - 5/8/2016
A Festival for May
Camlann Village - 10320 Kelly Rd NE - Carnation, WA
www.camlann.org   (425) 788-8624

Maypole dancing, arts and crafts, minstrels, and our famous May Feast.

Paid Admission
Kid Friendly Event

5/7/2016 - 5/7/2016
Seattle Reptile Expo
Evergreen State Fairgrounds - Monroe, WA
www.nwreptileexpos.com

Paid Admission
Kid Friendly Event
Hours: 10am - 5pm

Vendor Contact: reptileexpo@ymail.com

5/14/2016 - 5/14/2016
Backyard Wildlife Festival
Tukwila Community Center - Tukwila, WA
www.backyardwildlifefestival.org   (206) 768-2822

There's plenty to keep the whole family entertained at this event! Includes a Kids Garden Party area, speakers and local experts, arts & crafts vendors and native plant sales.

Free Admission
Kid Friendly Event
Hours: 9am - 3pm

Vendor Contact: Shanon Fisher
shannon.fisher@tukwilawa.gov

5/27/2016 - 5/30/2016
Family-A-Fair
Howell Canyon Estate - Onasket, WA

Admission: Not Provided

Vendor Contact: Derek Howell
# of Vendors: 14   Not a Juried Event

5/28/16 (tentative)
Kent Interntional Festival 2016
Kent Commons - Kent, WA
www.kentinternationalfestival.com (206) 601-6957

Free Admission   Kid Friendly Event
Hours: 7am - 10pm

Vendor Contact: Nancy Skipton
nancy@simplycelebrations.com   # of Vendors: 25

5/2016 - TBA
Auburn's Petpalooza 2016
Game Farm Park - 3030 R St SE
Auburn, WA
www.auburnwa.gov/things_to_do/community/pe
tpalooza_s_p205.htm?EventMode=View&EventOcc
urrence=0   (253) 931-3043

A special day for pet lovers and pets! The event kicks off
with a Dog Trot 3K/5K fun Run at 9:30 am. Petpalooza
features live entertainment, pony rides, an agility area,
pet contests, face painting and other children's activities,
150+ vendors, pet adoptions, exams, vaccinations and
more. Event is 10am-5pm at Game Farm Park.

Free Admission   Kid Friendly Event
Hours: 10am - 5pm

Vendor Contact: Kristy kpachciarz@auburnwa.gov
# of Vendors: 150

5/27/2016 – 5/30/2016
Northwest Folklife Festival
Seattle Center - 305 Harrison St – Seattle, WA
(206) 684-7300
www.nwfolklife.org

Festival blends traditional cultural expression and emerging art forms; hosting workshops, artisans and crafts market, sidewalk vendors, food vendors, live entertainment of the region's most accomplished professional and amateur musicians, family Discovery Zone, and more. Take a moment and relax in our beer garden, dance and enjoy the festivities, rain or shine! Enjoy an atmosphere that celebrates the diversity of the Northwest!

Donation Requested Admission
Kid Friendly Event

Vendor Contact: Katie McColgan Katie@nwfolklife.org
Deadline: Applications are accepted as follows
                 Craft Vendors Dec – Jan
                 Food Vendors Nov – Dec
                 Uncommon Market Jan – Feb
                 Sidewalk Vendor Feb – Mar

Attendance: 235,000

Buttercups in the August sunshine are like little cups of gold,
Dasies and sunflowers rise with bowing head towards the sun,
Violets of majestic blue creep within the shadow of the tree,
Butterflies dance from flower-to-flower,
Fluttering on the summer breeze and never a care in the world.
~~ Catherine Pittman © 2015

Spring being a tough act to follow, God created June.
~~ Al Bernstein, American Sportscaster

The Soul would have no rainbow if the eyes had no tears
~~American Indian Proverb Minquas Tribe

6/4/16 (tentative)
Evergreen Mountain Bike Festival 2016
Duthie Hill Park - Issaquah, WA
www.evergreenmtbfetival.com

Free Admission   Kid Friendly Event
Hours: 9am - 5pm

Vendor Contact: Brian Rivard
bryanr@evergreenmtb.org   # of Vendors: 40

6/10/2016 - 6/28/2016
Marysville Strawberry Festival 2016
Various Marysville Locations - Marysville, WA
www.maryfest.org   (360) 659-7664

Includes the Berry Fun Run/Walk, Talent Show, Vendor
Market at Asbery Field Park, beer garden, fashion show,
car show, shortcake eating contest, carnival at Marysville
Middle School , kiddies parade, grand parade, and
more!

Admission: Not Provided
Kid Friendly Event
Hours: See event schedule online

Vendor Contact: maryfest.org@gmail.com

---

*If a June night could talk, it would probably boast that it
invented romance.*
~~Bern Williams, Philosopher 1929 – 2003

*What is one to say about June, the time of perfect young
summer, the fulfillment of the promise of the earlier months,
and with as yet no sign to remind one that its fresh young
beauty will ever fade.*
~~ Gertrude Jekyll, British Writer 1843 – 1932

6/10/2016 - 6/12/2016
Sorticulture Garden Art Festival
Legion Memorial Park - Everett, WA
www.everettwa.gov/765/Festivals-Events
(425) 257-7107

This three day festival is filled with handmade garden art and plants from specialty nurseries. Also includes live music, display gardens, playhouse and free kids activities.

Free Admission   Kid Friendly Event
Hours: Fri: 10am-8pm;
        Sat: 10am-6pm; Sun: 10am-4pm

Vendor Contact: Lisa Newland
lnewland@everettwa.gov

6/11/16 (tentative)
Georgetown Carnival
Various - See website carnival map - Seattle, WA
www.georgetownmerchants.org/georgetown-carnival.html

Admission: Not Provided
Kid Friendly Event
Hours: Noon - 10pm

6/12/2016 - 6/12/2016
Annual Fleur de Lis Festival
Westport Winery - Westport, WA

Come enjoy the farm's 5,000 irises in bloom. Festival includes a French-style marketplace hosted by the Westport Art Festival.

Free Admission   Kid Friendly Event

Green was the silence, wet was the light,
The month of June trembled like a butterfly...
~~Pablo Neruda, Nobel Price Winner for Literature in 1971,
1904 - 1973

6/17/2016 - 6/19/2016
Fremont Street Summer Solstice Fair
Fremont Neighborhood: Fremont Ave on N 35th st - 34th St/Canal St - Seattle, WA
www.fremontfair.org

Paid Admission
Hours: Fri: 5pm-11pm;
        Sat: 10am-11pm;
        Sun: 11am-6pm

# of Vendors: 300

6/17/2016 - 6/19/2016
Meeker Days Festival
Downtown Puyallup - Puyallup, WA
(253) 840-2631

Admission: Not Provided
Kid Friendly Event
Hours: Fri: Noon - 9pm;
        Sat: 10am - 9pm; Sun: 10am - 5pm

Vendor Contact:
meekerdays@puyallupmainstreet.com
Deadline: March 2016
# of Years Held: 126

6/17/2016 - 6/17/2016
Morgan Junction Community Festival 2016
California Ave SW & Morgan St SW and Fauntleroy Way SW - Seattle, WA
www.morganjunction.org   (206) 651-4288

Free Admission
Kid Friendly Event
Hours: 10am - 6pm

Vendor Contact: Tod Rodman

6/17/16 (tentative)
Seattle Pet Expo
Washington State Convention Center - Seattle, WA
www.seattlepetexpo.com   (800) 977-3609, ext 108

Free Admission
# of Vendors: 190+

6/19/2016 - 6/19/2016
Fenders on Front Street
Front Street - Issaquah, WA
www.fendersonfrontstreet.com   (425) 391-1112

Admission: Not Provided
Kid Friendly Event
Hours: 7am - 3pm

Vendor Contact: info@fendersonfrontstreet.com

6/24/2016 - 6/26/16 (tentative)
Recycled Arts Festival 2016
Esther Short Park - Vancouver, WA
www.recycledartsfestival.com

This huge family-friendly event hosts recycled arts and crafts, local music, family fun activities and more!

Admission: Not Provided
Kid Friendly Event

Vendor Contact: Sally Fisher
sally.fisher@clark.wa.gov
Deadline: 3/31/16

# of Years Held: 11

It was June, and the world smelled of roses. The sunshine was like powdered gold over the grassy hillside.
~~Maud Hart Lovelace, Betsy-Tacy and Tib Series, 1941
1892 - 1980

06/19/16 (Tentative)
Edmonds Arts Festival
700 Main St – Edmonds, WA
www.edmondartsfestival.com   (425) 771-6421

Admission: Not Provided
Kid Friendly Event

# of Vendors: 240
Juried Event

6/24/2016 - 6/26/2016
Rusty Scupper's Pirate Daze
Westport Docks - Westport, WA

Pirates invade Westport for a wonderful weekend of fun, food and frivolity! Dress up in your finest pirate outfit, and shop, dance, interact and enjoy Rusty Scupper and his band of buccaneers!

Admission: Not Provided
Kid Friendly Event

Daisy Pollen Flower ©
PDPhotos
All Free Download

What is a perfect summer day?
It is seeing the bright blue summer sky,
Hearing the melodies of nature all sing in harmony,
And feeling the sweet summer sun upon my face.
These are the joys of the perfect summer day!
~~Catherine Pittman © 2015

Eastside Heritage Center's
Strawberry Festival
in BELLEVUE

www.bellevuestrawberryfestival.org

6/25/2016 - 6/26/2015
Bellevue Strawberry Festival
Crossroads Park - Bellevue, WA
(425) 450-1049

Features family entertainment, fresh strawberry shortcake,hands-on history experiences, food and vendor booths, music, games, an auto show and more!

EASTSIDE
HERITAGE
CENTER
Discover. Share. Participate.

Presented by the Eastside Heritage Center.

Free Admission
Kid Friendly Event
Hours: Sat: 10am - 8pm; Sun: 10am - 6pm

Vendor Contact:
info@bellevuestrawberryfestival.org
Deadline: 4/30/15   Attendance: 45000

6/25/2016 - 6/26/2016
Midsomer Festival
Camlann Village - 10320 Kelly Rd NE - Carnation, WA
www.camlann.org   (425) 788-8624

The Lord of Camlann invites you to attend the Midsommer Festival! Featuring summer games, puppetry, magic shows, arts and crafts, archery and minstrels!

Paid Admission   Kid Friendly Event

6/24/2016 – 6/26/2016
Taste of Tacoma®
Point Defiance Park – Tacoma, WA
(253) 759-8272 or (425) 295-3262
www.tasteoftacoma.com

- Taste a little bit of everything with the Just A Bite items for $3.75 or less!
- Live cooking interactive entertainment
- Wine Tasting
- Craft Beer asting
- Five Outdoor Stages featuring all genres of music, including a Family Fun Kids Stage
- The Funtastic Carnival offering rides and games for kids and parents too!
- Handcrafted and Commercial Vendors, including handmade candles, phtographs, artwork, metalworks and more! We've broght ogether some of the Northwest's most alended artisans and crafters

Free Admission
Kid Friendly Event
Hours: Friday & Saturday, 11am – 9pm
　　　　Sunday, 11am – 8pm

Vendor Contact: carlyo@festivals-inc.com or
　　　　　　　　(425) 295-3262, ext 110
# of Vendors: 100+
Deadline: March 2016

Attendance: 250,000+
# of Years: 31

The perfect summer's day is when the sun is shining, the wind is blowing, the birds are singing, and the lawn mower is broken.
~~James Dent, American Author & Sportswriter

06/2016 - TBA
FLY-IN
Dallesport/Murdock fire department fundraiser
45 Airport Way - Dallesport, WA
www.facebook.com/pages/Columbia...Fly-In/801910713218401
541-993-1138

This fundraiser is to help the Dallesport/Murdock Fire Department. Event will be a blast and the kids will have fun! Featuring:
~Classic Planes & Cars
~Scenic Flights
~Military Planes Fun Jumpers Auction
~Inflatable Jumpers
~Air Brush tattoos
~Cotton Candy Vendors
~Snow Cones
~Fire Department Spray house (kids help put out fire; painted board with doors opening with painted flames. Not a real Fire)
~Fire Trucks
~Breakfast & Lunch.
~More to be added as it gets closer.

*Want to be a vendor?
 Call Rhet Howard for further information.
*Anyone with Classic Cars is welcome to show them off.

Admission: Not Provided
Kid Friendly Event
Hours: Saturday 7am to 5pm

Vendor Contact: Rhet Howard: (541) 993-1138
Not a Juried Event

Mountains

Skiing

Kite Flying　　Rock Climbing

Beaches

Hiking　　# Attractions

Waterfalls

Sand Dunes

Fishing

Whale Watching　　Snowboarding

Horseback Riding

Camping

Surfing # Family Fun

Bowling　Miniature Golf

Skating

River Rafting

Amusement Parks

1909 Looff Carrousel
507 N Howard Spokane, WA
www.spokaneriverfrontpark.com/ (509) 625-6601

Admission: Not Provided

7 Wonders Museum
4749 Spirit Lake Hwy Silverlake, WA
www.creationism.org/sthelens

Admission: Not Provided

A Place to Play for Kids
55 Spring St Friday Harbor, WA
www.aplacetoplay.biz   (360) 378-0378

Indoor creative and imaginative play just for kids to play
and parents to relax!

Paid Attraction

Absolute Air Park
18802 67th Ave NE Arlington, WA
www.absoluteairpark.com   (855) 788-JUMP

Hours: Mon: 3pm-9pm; Wed-Thur: 3pm-9pm; Fri:
Noon-Midnight; Sat: 10am - Midnight; Sun: 10am-8pm.
Wild Child Alley (ages 2-5): Mon/Wed/Thur: 5pm-8pm;
Fri/Sat/Sun:2pm-8pm

Paid Attraction

African-American Museum of Washington
926 Court C Tacoma, WA
www.neamnw.org   (206) 518-6000

Hours: Wed: 11am-5pm; Thurs: 11am-7pm; Fri-Sun: 11am-5pm. Closed Monday & Tuesday

The chronical of the struggles of the Northwest's Affrican Americans.

Paid Admission

Anacortes Kayak Tours
2201 Skyline Way Ste 203 Anacortes, WA
www.anacorteskayaktours.com   (800) 992-1801

Paid Attraction

Arcade-ia
527 E Main St Walla Walla, WA
www.facebook.com/wwarcadeia?fref=ts
(509) 876-4208

Admission: Not Provided

Argosy Cruises & Tillicum Village
1101 Alaskan Way - Pier 55, Suite 201 Seattle, WA
Hours: See website for hours and rates
www.argosycruises.com   (206) 623-1445

Experience the Northwest's tribal culture when you cruise to historic Blake Island and visit Tillicum Village. Enjoy steamed clams, watch salmon cook over open fires and enjoy a wonderful salmon bake. See Native American dances, artwork and hear the stories of the village. A 4-hour cruise & adventure.

Paid Admission

Bellingham Sportsplex
1225 Civic Field Way Bellingham, WA
www.bellinghamsportsplex.com   (360) 676-1919

Paid Attraction

Bicycle Adventures
28699 SE High Point Issaquah, WA
www.bicycleadventures.com   (800) 443-6060

Paid Attraction

Bill Speidel's Underground Tour
608 1st Ave Seattle, WA
www.undergroundtour.com/   (206) 682-4646

Hours: April - September: Daily, 9am - 7pm;
        June - August: extended hours.
        October - March, 10am-6pm.
        Christmas week hours: 9am-6pm.

This unique tour is a fun way to learn the history of Seattle. After the great fire of Seattle in 1889, the city was rebuilt on top of the ruins. The 1 1/2 hour tour explores the underground passage that once were the main roads and storefronts of Seattle's downtown. Moderately rugged terrain, so be sure that you and the kids wear solid walking shoes!

Admission: Not Provided

Birch Bay Waterslides
4874 Birch Bay Lynden Rd Blaine, WA
Hours: Closed winter months
www.birchbaywaterslides.net/   (360) 371-7500

Admission: Not Provided

Blackman House Museum
118 Avenue B Snohomish, WA
www.snohomishhistoricalsociety.org/
(360) 568-5235

Admission: Not Provided

Bremerton Childrens Bug & Reptile Museum
1118 Charleston Beach rd W,
Bremerton, WA 98312
Bremerton, WA
www.BugMuseum.com

Hours: Every day 10-5

See our cool LIVE bugs, explore bizarre bugs under the microscope, look through glasses that let you see like a bug, and even watch busy ants in our giant 8 foot long Ant Farm! We have the weirdest and most interesting bugs on display for you to see up close. See fascinating LIVE Reptiles from around the world UP CLOSE AND PERSONAL. Over 15 kid friendly exhibits to explore.

Free Admission

Burke Museum of Natural History & Culture
17th Ave NE & NE 45th Seattle, WA
www.burkemuseum.org   (206) 543-5590

Hours: Daily, 10am - 5pm
Paid Attraction

Cat Tales
17020 Newport Hwy Mead, WA
Closed All Mondays.
www.cattales.org   (509) 238-4126

Hours: Summer (May - Sept): Tues - Sun 10am - 6pm;
            Winter (Oct - Apr): Tues - Sun 10am - 4pm.

"Come see what all the roaring is about" at Cat Tales
Zoo!   Hand feed the animals (8 years & over),
experience the rare opportuniting to get up close and
personal with a tiger, bear or royal white tiger!

Paid Admission

Charlie's Safari
5400 Martin Way E Lacey, WA
www.charliessafari.com   (360) 292-1600

Hours: Mon - Thurs: 11am-8pm; Fri: 11am-9pm;
            Sat: 10am-9pm; Sun: 11am-8pm

Paid Attraction

Cheney Historical Museum
420 1st St Cheney, WA
www.cheneymuseum.org/   (509) 235-2202

Admission: Not Provided

Cherry Hill Family Golf Course
530 Cherry Hill Rd Granger, WA
www.grangergolf.com/   (509) 854-1800

Admission: Not Provided

Children's Museum of Skagit County
550 Cascade Mall Dr Burlington, WA
www.skagitchildrensmuseum.net   (360) 757-8888

Hours: Monday - Saturday, 10am-5pm;
        Sunday: Noon - 5pm.
        Toddler Tuesday's 8:30 am - 10am

Children learn through play and exploration and this museum is designed just for them, providing a playful, interactive environment and learning experience.

Admission: Not Provided

Children's Museum of Skagit County
550 Cascade Mall Dr Burlington, WA
www.skagitchildrensmuseum.net   (360) 757-8888

Community free day is the second Tuesday each month. Other activities include: Highland fun & Games, Summer Camps, Preschool Museum Explorers, Movie Night at the Museum.

Admission: Not Provided

Children's Museum of Spokane
808 W Main Ave Spokane, WA
www.mobiusspokane.org   (509) 321-7121

Hours: Tues - Sat: 10am-5pm;
        Sun: 11am-5pm. Closed Monday.
        See website for exceptions for events or
        reserved parties.

Hands-on museum for kids.
Admission: Not Provided

Children's Museum of Tacoma
936 Broadway Tacoma, WA
www.playtacoma.org   (253) 627-6031
Hours: Wednesday - Sunday, 10am - 5pm.
        Closed Tuesday.

Featuring hands-on exhibits that make learning fun!
Admission: Not Provided

Clark County Historical Museum
1511 Main St Vancouver, WA
www.cchmuseum.org/

Admission: Not Provided

Cougar Mountain Zoo
19525 SE 54th St Issaquah, WA
www.cougarmountainzoo.org   (425) 391-5508

Hours: Jan - Nov: Wed - Sun, 9:30 am - dusk;
        Dec Hours: Daily, 10am - 4:30 pm
Paid Attraction

Crystal Mountain Ski Resort
33914 Crystal Mountain Blvd Crystal Mountain, WA
www.crystalmountainresort.com   (888) 754-6199

Includes runs for all levels and skiing skills.
Admission: Not Provided

Deep Forest Challenge
5400 N Pearl St Tacoma, WA
www.deepforestchallenge.com

Paid Attraction

Dizzy Castle
11606 NE 66th St Vancouver, WA
Hours: Daily, 9am-8pm
www.dizzycastle.com   (360) 885-7529

Indoor playground featuring massive castle and pirate
ship play structure, dueling air cannons, snake pit,
slides, and much more. Features an upscale Café for
mom and dad. Complimentary iPads to use in a relaxed
area. Mini play areas for toddlers.
Admission: Not Provided

Dream Playground
Erickson Park on Race St Port Angeles, WA
www.padreamplayground.org
Hours: Open year round

This is one of the collest playgrounds. It has a creative
twist to the standard swings, slids and climbing
equipment, and has beautiful surroundings. Includes a
climbing wall, slides of all kinds, playhouses, picnic area,
skateboard park, and tennis courts. It is the perfect
place for a family picnic and kids play area!

Admission: Not Provided

Dungeness Spit National Wildlife Refuge
Kitchen-Dick Rd Sequim, WA
www.visitsun.com/dungeness.html
(360) 683-5847

Located on the north coast of the Olympic Peninsula, just
west of Sequim. The refuge is over 5 miles long, and is
one of the world's longest natural sand spits that grows
about 13 feet every year. Incredible wildlife and also a
historic lighthouse.

Free Attraction

DuPont Historical Museum
207 Barksdale Ave DuPont, WA
www.dupontmuseum.com/   (253) 964-2399

Admission: Not Provided

Echo Valley Ski Area
1700 Cooper Gulch Rd Chelan, WA
Hours: See website - dependent upon SNOW!
www.echovalley.org   (509) 682-4002

Offers skiing and snow tubing.

Admission: Not Provide

Edmonds Historical Museum
118 5th Ave N Edmonds, WA
www.historicedmonds.org/   (425) 774-0900

Admission: Not Provided

Elevated Sportz Ultimate Trampoline Park & Event Center
18311 Bothell Everett Hwy
Bothell, WA
www.elevatedsportz.com
(425) 949-4488

Hours: Mon - Thur: 10am - 9pm; Fri: 10am - 10pm;
Sat: 10am-11pm; Sun: 10am-9pm

Located in Bothell (20 mins north of Seattle), Elevated Sportz is a premier indoor trampoline park and event center offers hours of recreation fun for the entire family, and fab amenities for parents. This place is very popular with a colossal-sized four-story indoor play castle and four premium trampoline courts including a main jumping court, 3-D dodgeball court, basketball slam dunk court, and trampoline foam pit. Laser Maze challenge and EyePlay interative games also keeps the kiddos busy.

Paid Attraction

EMP Museum
325 5th Ave N Seattle, WA
www.empmuseum.org
Hours: Open Daily, 10am - 7pm

From Bugs Bunny animation to Star Wars™ or exploring infinite worlds of science fiction, this fun, interactive museum provides a wealth of learning opportunities for the entire family!

Paid Admission

Flying Heritage Collection
3407 109th St SW Everett, WA
www.flyingheritage.com/   (206) 342-4242
Admission: Not Provided

Fort Walla Walla Museum
755 Myra Rd Walla Walla, WA
www.fortwallawallamuseum.org/   (509) 525-7703

Admission: Not Provided

Ft. Vancouver National Park
750 Anderson St Vancouver, WA
www.fortvan.org   (360) 992-1800

Free Attraction

Funland
200 S Pacific Long Beach, WA
https://funbeach.com/other-businesses/funland-inc/   (360) 642-2223

Admission: Not Provided

Future of Flight Aviation Center & Boeing Tour
8415 Paine Field Blvd Everett, WA
www.futureofflight.org/   (425) 438-8100

Your family's opportunity to explore the future and present of flight at this public tour at Boeing.

Admission: Not Provided

Hands On Children's Museum
Olympia, WA
www.hocm.org   (360) 956-0818

Hours: Tues - Sat: 10am-5pm;
        Sun - Mon: 11am-5pm.
        Art & Sciences Activities run 11am 3pm;
        Outdoor Discover Center closes at 4:30 pm
        (sept-Mar) and 5pm (apr - Aug)

Paid Attraction; Free for Members

Harbor History Museum
4121 Harborview Dr Gig Harbor, WA
www.harborhistorymuseum.org   (253) 858-6722
Hours: Tues - Sun: 10am-5pm. Closed Mondays.

Paid Attraction

Hibulb Cultural Center & Natural History Preserve
6410 23rd Ave NE Tulalip, WA
www.hibulbculturalcenter.org/   (360) 716-2600

Admission: Not Provided

Hoh Rain Forest
Olympic National Park Port Angeles, WA
www.olympicpeninsula.org/things-to-do/hoh-rain-forest   (360) 374-6925

Visit Olympic National Park for a day with nature!.
Free Attraction

Hot Rod Gallery Museum
17520 147th St SE Monroe, WA
www.hotrod-gallery.com/   (425) 224-5009

Admission: Not Provided

Hyak Sno-Park Sledding Hill
Off Exit 54, I-90 Easton, WA
www.snowrec.org/#!sno-parks/c20nd

Parking pass required. Area provides a smaller slope for the under 5 crowd, and a larger slope for older kids and adults. Beautiful scenery. Restrooms provided, but no food or snack bars.

Free Attraction

Icicle Village Resort
565 Hwy 2 Leavenworth, WA
www.iciclevillage.com/play   (800) 961-0162

Paid Attraction

Imagine Children's Museum
1502 Wall St Everett, WA
www.imaginecm.org   (425) 258-1006
Hours: Tues/Wed: 9am-5pm; Thur - Sat: 10am - 5pm;
          Sun: 11am - 5pm. Closed Monday's

Paid Attraction

Island Adventures Whale Watching
1801 Commercial Ave Anacortes, WA
www.island-adventures.com   (800) 465-4604

Paid Attraction

Issaquah Salmon Hatchery
125 W Sunset Way Issaquah, WA
www.issaquahfish.org/   (425) 392-1118

Admission: Not Provided

JJ Jump
7500 NE 16th Ave #2-D Vancouver, WA
www.jjjump.com/locations/vancouver
(360) 213-2524

Paid Attraction

Job Carr Cabin Museum
2350 N 30th St Tacoma, WA
www.jobcarrmuseum.org   (253) 627-5405

Museum pays tribute to the original Euro-American
settlers.

Admission: Donations Welcome

Jump Around Fun Zone
4600 Guide Meridian Bellingham, WA
www.jumparoundfunzone.com   (360) 647-5867
Hours: Wed - Sun: 10am - 7pm.
            Closed Monday & Tuesday

Paid Attraction

Jumpin' Jelly Beanz
16 E Poplar St Walla Walla, WA
www.jumpinjellybeanz.com   (509) 200-4958

Paid Admission

K1 Speed Seattle
2207 NE Bel-Red Rd Redmond, WA
Hours: Open Daily. Mon - Thurs, 12pm-10pm; Fri,
11am-11pm; Sat, 10am-11pm; Sun 10am-8pm.
www.k1speed.com   (425) 455-9999

Indoor go-cart racing.
Admission: Not Provided

Kangaroo Cottage
Monroe, WA
www.monroefunnyfarm.com   (360) 863-0280

Admission: Not Provided

Kent Valley Ice Centre
6015 S 240th St Kent, WA
www.kentvalleyicecentre.com   (253) 850-2400

Paid Attraction

KidsQuest Children's Museum
4091 Factoria Square Mall SE Bellevue, WA
www.kidsquestmuseum.org   (425) 637-8100
Hours: Wed & Sat: 10am-5pm; Thu & Fri: 10am-8pm;
            Sun: 12pm-5pm Closed Mondays

Paid Admission

Kirkman House Museum
214 N Colville Walla Walla, WA
www.kirkmanhousemuseum.org/   (509) 529-4373

Admission: Not Provided

Lake Whatcom Railway
5100 Wickersham St Wickersham, WA
www.lakewhatcomrailway.com   (360) 441-0719
Hours: See the online calendar

You and your family are invited to ride an authentic, full-sized old Northern Pacific train! See oassebger coaches from the 1900's, and ancient wooden freight cars. This is the friendliest excursion railroad and worth the 1 1/2 hour trip! Some come aboard for a lot of fun!

Admission: Not Provided

Lewis County Historical Museum
599 NW Front Way Chehalis, WA
www.lewiscountymuseum.org/   (360) 748-0831

Admission: Not Provided

Longmire Mineral Hotsprings
Longmire, WA

A great place to soak those tired muscles. Located near the Longmire Campgrounds.

Free Attraction

Longmire Museum
Tahoma Woods Star Route Longmire, WA
(360) 569-2111

Showcases local history for the region.
Admission: Not Provided

Loup Loup Skiing
Between Twisp & Okanogan on Hwy 20, WA
Twisp   (509) 557-3405

Great tube slide in addition to outstanding skiing. There is fun for the entire family.

Admission: Not Provided

Lynnwood Ice Center
19803 68th Ave W Lynnwood, WA
www.lynnwoodicecenter.com   (425) 640-9999
Hours: See website calendar

Paid Attraction

Makah Cultural & Research Center
1880 Bay View Ave Neah Bay, WA
www.makahmuseum.com   (360) 645-2711
Hours: Open daily, 10am-5pm. Closed Thanksgiving,
          Christmas and New Year's Day

Showcases the Makah culture with 300 - 500 year old artifacts on exhibit.

Admission: Not Provided

Marymere Falls Trail
Marymere Fall/Lake Crescent Port Angeles, WA
www.olympicpeninsulawaterfalltrail.com/marymere-falls

A winding hike to a breathtaking waterfall. It's an easy short hike for children with just enough level ground and steep climbing to make it a fun hike. Turn of the gizmos and gadgets, and enjoy the outdoors!

Free Attraction

McAllister Museum of Aviation

2008 S 16th Ave Yakima, WA

www.mcallistermuseum.org   (598) 457-4933

Hours: Open year round, Thurs & Fri: 10am - 4pm;
        Saturday: 9am - 4pm.

Admission: Not Provided

Meadowbrook Family Fun Center

7200 W Nob Hill Blvd Yakima, WA

www.yakimafamilyfun.com   (509) 966-3836

Hours: Fall Hours: Outdoor activities 11am - 8pm;
        Arcade: 11am-9pm.
        See website for specific activities' hours.

Paid Attraction

Miniature World Family Fun Center

4620 Birch Bay Lynden Rd Blaine, WA

www.miniatureworld.org   (360) 371-7700

Paid Attraction

Moments in Time Trail

Olympic National Park Port Angeles, WA

(800) 833-6388

This hike is just under 1 mile, and provides you marvelous view of Crescent lake, old homestead sites and the surrounding beautiful forest. Hike is appropriate for ages 6 & up.

Free Attraction

Morton Historic Railroad Depot

194 E Main Ave Morton, WA

www.visitmorton.com/   (360) 496-0070

Admission: Not Provided

Mt. Ranier Scenic Railroad
54124 Mountain Hwy E Elbe, WA
www.mrsr.com/   (360) 492-5588

Admission: Not Provided

Mt. Spokane Skiing
29500 N Mt. Spokane Park Dr Mead, WA
www.mtspokane.com   (509) 238-2220

Day and night skiing. Daycare available.
Admission: Not Provided

Museum of Flight
9404 E Marginal Way S Seattle, WA
www.museumofflight.org/   (206) 764-5720
Hours: Open 7 days a week, 10am - 5pm.
            Free First Thursdays from 5pm - 9pm

One of the largest air & space museums in the world,
provides a collection of over 150 historically significant
air and spacecraft. See a fighter plane, first Air Force
One, a Blackbird spy plane.

Paid Attraction

Museum of History & Industry
860 Terry Ave N Seattle, WA
www.mohai.org   (206) 324-1126
Hours: Daily, 10am-5pm;
            expanded to 8pm on Thursday's

Kids will have a blast with the many interactive exhibits
at this museum. The MOHAI museum will not
disappoint, and the whole family will enjoy the
surrounding setting as well as the museum.

Admission: Not Provided

Nisqually National Wildlife Refuge
100 Brown Farm Rd Olympia, WA
www.fws.gov/refuge/nisqually/   (360) 753-9467
Hours: Trails open daily from sunrise to sunset.

Admission: Not Provided

North Cascades National Park
810 State Route 20 Sedro Woolley, WA

The North Cascades are relatively new mountains, glaciers and streams, and lie near the dynamic interface of tectonic plates. It is a great opportunity to study geologic processes unfolding. A great way to spend the day exploring nature and hiking the lakes and streams.

Free Attraction

Northern Pacific Railway Museum
10 S Asotin Ave Toppenish, WA
www.nprymuseum.org   (509) 865-1911
Hours: 2015:
          Open thru October 15, Tues - Sat, 10am - 4pm;
          Sun Noon - 4. Closed Monday's.
          After October 15, closed until May 1, 2016.
          Regularly opened May 1 - October 15 each year.

Paid Attraction

Northwest African American Museum
2300 S Massachusetts St Seattle, WA
www.naamnw.org   (206) 518-6000
Hours: Wed/Fri-Sun: 11am-5pm;
          Thur: 11am-7pm. Closed Monday & Tuesday.

Paid Attraction

Northwest Carriage Museum
314 Alder St Raymond, WA
www.nwcarriagemuseum.org   (360) 942-4150

Introduce your kids to how people use to travel at this unique museum! The museum is home to beautifully restored horse-drawn vehicles. Many of the carriages in the museum were considered the cadillacs of their day.

Admission: Not Provided

Northwest Trek Wildlife Park
11610 Trek Dr E Eatonville, WA
www.nwtrek.org/   (360) 832-6117

Admission: Not Provided

Olympic Flight Museum
7637 A Old Hwy 99 SE Olympia, WA
www.olympicflightmuseum.com   (360) 705-3925
Hours: Fall & Winter: Wed - Sun, 11am - 5pm.
          Closed Monday & Tuesday
Paid Attraction

Olympic Game Farm
1423 Ward Rd Sequim, WA
Hours: Daily, 9am - 4pm
www.olygamefarm.com   (800) 778-4295

Paid Attraction

Olympic Peninsula Adventures
83 Medsker Rd Sequim, WA
www.olympicpeninsulaadventures.com/
(360) 775-1102

Admission: Not Provided

Orcas Island Historical Museum
181 N Beach Rd Eastsound, WA
www.orcasmuseum.org   (360) 376-4849

Paid Admission

Orcas Island Trail Rides
Moran State Park - South End Camp Olga, WA
Hours: Hours: 10:30 or 1pm
www.orcastrailrides.com   (360) 376-2134

Come visit Orcas Island Trail Rides and ride with us in an old growth forest on Orcas Island. The rides are awesome--the best in the Northwest, as many of our customers have told us who ride everywhere they travel. You can ride all the way to the top of the mountain and see a view of the San Juans, or ride through the old growth forest--passing a waterfall on all the rides. Call soon for reservations--we are open year around. 360-376-2134

Paid Attraction

Orting Bike Trail
Orting, WA

The trail is flat for the majority of the way, and is great for biking and roller blading. It is well worth the trek and includes other activities, such as fishing and picknicking.

Free Attraction

Outer Island Excursions
Eastsound, WA
www.outerislandx.com   (360) 376-3711

Paid Attraction

Pacific Science Center
200 Second Ave N Seattle, WA
www.pacificsciencecenter.org   (206) 443-2001

Paid Admission

Pavilion Amusement Rides
507 N Howard Spokane, WA
www.spokaneriverfrontpark.com/ (509) 625-6601

Admission: Not Provided

Pike Place Market
1st Ave & Pike St Seattle, WA
www.pikeplacemarket.org   (206) 682-7453
Hours: Breakfast: 6am; Produce & Seafood: 7am;
            Crafts Market: 10am - 4pm;
            Merchant Hours: 10am-6pm;
            Restaurants: 6am - 1:30 am (varies).
            Closed Thanksgiving & Christmas Day

Crafts Market, Farmers Market, Fish Market and more!
Free Admission

Pioneer Farm Museum & Ohop Indian Village
7716 Ohop Valley Rd E Eatonville, WA
www.pioneerfarmmuseum.org
- Spring Hours: March 15 - Fathers Day, Sat & Sun 11am-4pm;
- Summer Hours: Fathers Day - Labor Day Weekend, Daily 11am-4pm;
- Fall Hours: Labor Day - Thanksgiving, Sat & Sun 11am-4pm;
- Winter Hours: Closed until March 15

This museum will be a hit with the whole family! Visit farm animals, learn how to milk a cow, gather chicken eggs. There are short horse rides, blacksmith and carpentry shops, old log cabins, and more. It's a hands-on tour of pioneer life that is not to be missed!

Admission: Not Provided

Play Indoor Playground & Learning Center
5934 State Hwy 303 NE Bremerton, WA
www.playkitsap.com   (360) 479-7529
Current Hours: Mon/Tues/Fri: 9:30am - 5pm;
             Wed/Thur: 9:30am-7pm;
             Sat: 9:30am-3pm.
             Closed Sundays.

Paid Attraction

Point Defiance Zoo & Aquarium
5400 N Pearl St Tacoma, WA
Hours: Open Daily, 9:30am - 5pm.
www.pdza.org   (253) 591-5337

This wonderful zoo not only features animals, but has an
excellent aquarium, a fun riding carousel and new kids
play area exhibit.   Admission discounts available for
Pierce County residents, military and AAA members.

Admission: Not Provided

Polson History Museum
1611 Riverside Ave Hoquiam, WA
www.polsonmuseum.org   (360) 533-5862
Hours: Wed - Sat: 11-4; Sun: 12-4.
        Closed Monday, Tuesday & National Holidays

Paid Attraction

Red Rooster Route Family Farm Fun
Off exit 208 from I-5 Arlington, WA
www.redroosterroute.com/   (360) 435-6516

Admission: Not Provided

Remlinger Farms Tours
32510 NE 32nd St Carnation, WA
www.remlingerfarms.com/tours.htm
(425) 333-4135

Admission: Not Provided

Ride the Ducks
516 Broad St Seattle, WA
www.ridetheducksofseattle.com/   (206) 441-3825

No trip is complete without riding this WWII amphibious landing craft! It is one of Seattle's must-see activities.

Paid Attraction

San Juan Historical Museum
405 Price St Friday Harbor, WA
www.sjmuseum.org   (360) 378-3949
Hours: Oct & Apr: Saturday, 1-4;
         May - September: Wed - Sat, 10am - 4pm and
         Sunday, 1pm-4pm.
         November through March via appointment only

A must-see attraction as you and your family explor Friday Harbor in the San Juan Islands.

Admission: Not Provided

San Juan Island Whale & Wildlife Tours
2 Front St Friday Harbor, WA
www.sanjuanislandwhales.com/   (360) 298-0012

Admission: Not Provided

School of Acrobatics & New Circus Arts
674 S Orcas St Seattle, WA
Hours: See Website
www.sancaseattle.org   (206) 652-4433

Paid Admission

Science Center of Spokane
808 W Main Ave Spokane, WA
www.moiusspokane.org   (509) 321-7133
Hours: Tues - Sat: 10am-5pm;
        Sun: 11am-5pm.
        Closed Monday.
        See website for exceptions for events or
        reserved parties.

Exhibits for flight & engineering, space, the human body,
bio and physics labs, and more!

Admission: Not Provided

Seattle Aquarium
1483 Alaskan Way Seattle, WA
www.seattleaquarium.org/   (206) 386-4300

Admission: Not Provided

Seattle Art Museum
1300 1st Ave Seattle, WA
www.visitsam.org/   (206) 654-3210

Paid Attraction

Seattle Center
305 Harrison St Seattle, WA
www.seattlecenter.com

A large complex in downtown Seattle, which features the
Children's Museum, Pacific Science Center, Space Needle
and a small amusement park.

Admission: Not Provided

Seattle Chinese Garden
6000 16th Ave SW Seattle, WA
www.seattlechinesegarden.org   (206) 934-5219

The hilltop gardens features a traditional Chinese
courtyard, pavilion, and plants.

Admission: Not Provided

Seattle Waterfront Harbor Sightseeing Tour Cruise
1101 Alaskan Way - Pier 55 Seattle, WA
http://www.argosycruises.com

Admission: Not Provided

Sidney Museum & Arts
202 Sidney Ave Port Orchard, WA
www.sidneymuseumandarts.com   (360) 876-3693

This national and state historic site houses artistic
treasures by renowned and emerging artists.

Free Admission

Sky Ride Over the Falls
507 N Howard Spokane, WA
www.spokaneriverfrontpark.com/   (509) 625-6601

Admission: Not Provided

Slater Museum of Natural History
University of Puget Sound - 1500 N Warner St
Tacoma, WA
Hours: Open Mon - Fri
www.pugetsound.edu/academics/academic-
resources/slater-museum/
(253) 879-3356

Shocasing bird, mammal, reptile, amphibian and plant
specimens from the Pacific Northwest

Paid Admissio

Slide Waters Lake Chelan Slidepark
102 Waterslide Dr Chelan, WA
www.slidewaterswaterpark.com   (509) 682-5751
Hours: Memorial Day - Labor Day, Daily 10am - Closing.
        Closing is 7pm from July until end of season.

Paid Attraction

Sol Duc Falls Trail
Olympic National Park Port Angeles, WA
www.olympicpeninsulawaterfalltrail.com

These falls are one of the most photographed falls in the
Olympic National Park.   Once you see it, you'll
understand why! The hike is an easy hike for kids, with
quaint little stream crossings.   The hike is just under 1
mile.

Free Attraction

Splash Down
3724 E 61st Ave Spokane, WA
www.spokanecounty.org/parks   (509) 448-5090

Admission: Not Provided

Splash Down Family Waterpark
11123 E Mission Ave Spokane Valley, WA
www.splashdownwaterpark.net   (509) 924-3079
Hours: Late May thr Labor Day. M - F 11am - 6pm;
        Sat: 11am - 6pm; Sun: Noon - 6pm

Paid Attraction

Surf 'n Slide Water Park
Dogwood St & 4th Ave Moses Lake, WA
www.mlrec.com/aquatic_center.html
(509) 764-3842

Admission: Not Provided

Sykart Indoor Racing Center (Washington)
17450 W Valley Hwy Tukwila, WA
www.sykart.com   (425) 251-5060
Hours: Mon - Sat: 11am - 11pm;
        Sun: 11am - 10pm

Paid Attraction

The Aberdeen Museum of History
111 E Third St Aberdeen, WA
www.aberdeen-museum.org   (360) 533-1976
Hours: Tues - Sat: 10am-5pm;
        Sun 12pm - 4pm Closed Mondays

Admission: Suggested Donation

The Bug Museum & Gift Shop
1118 Charleston Beach Rd W Bremerton, WA
Hours: Daily, 10am - 5pm
www.bugmuseum.com   (360) 373-7691

Paid Attraction

The Country Village
23718 Bothell-Everett Hwy Bothell, WA
www.countryvillagebothell.com   (425) 402-9818

Meandering paths will lead you and your family through
a whimsical world of trains, duckponds, one-of-a-kind
toys, shops, restaurants and more!

Admission: Not Provided

The Funhouse Commons
30 Pea Patch Lane Eastsound, WA
www.thefunhouse.org/   (360) 376-7177

Admission: Not Provided

The Little Farm at Windwater
20621 SE Green Valley Rd Auburn, WA
www.thelittlefarmatwindwater.com
(253) 929-6357

Hours: By appointment only. Great for playgroups
Admission: Not Provided

The Outback Kangaroo Farm
10030 State Route 530 NE Arlington, WA
www.outbackkangaroofarm.com   (360) 403-7474
Hours: Open March - October.
        Tour Leaves: Wed-Sun, 10am, Noon, 2pm, 4pm.
        Closed Monday & Tuesday.
        Available by Appointment only for groups of 11
        or more from November - February.

Admission: Not Provided

The Pottery Bug
4904 N Harvard Rd Ste 1 - 2 Otis Orchards, WA
www.potterybugstudio.com   (509) 891-0074

Paid Attraction

The Railroad-Depot History Museum
105 10th Ave Ritzville, WA
www.museums.goritzville.com/depot.php
(509) 659-1656
Hours: Memorial Day - Labor Day or by Appointment:
        Tues – Sat, 12pm-4pm.

Paid Attraction

The Rootbeer Store Tastings
20015 Hwy 99 Ste G Lynnwood, WA
www.therootbeerstore.com   (425) 673-9999

Admission: Not Provided

The State Capital Museum
211 21st Ave SW Olympia, WA
www.washingtonhistory.org   (360) 753-2580

Located in the historic Lord Mansion, the museum
features Native American history.

Paid Attraction

The Whale Museum
Friday Harbor Marine Ares Friday Harbor, WA
www.whalemuseum.org   (360) 378-4710
Oct - Memorial Day Weekend: Daily, 10am-4pm;
Jun - Sept: daily, 9am - 6pm

Paid Attraction

Tiffany's Skate Roller Skating & Family Fun Center
1113 N Meridian Puyallup, WA
www.skatetiffanys.com   (253) 848-1153

Paid Attraction

Traxx Indoor Racing
4329 Chennault Beach Rd Mukilteo, WA
Hours: Sun - Thurs: 11am-11pm; Fri-Sat: 10am - 1am.
www.traxxracing.com   (425) 493-8729

Paid Attraction

Veterans Memorial Museum
100 SW Veterans Way Chehalis, WA
www.veteransmuseum.org/   (360) 740-8875

Admission: Not Provided

Washington State History Museum
1911 Pacific Ave Tacoma, WA
www.washingtonhistory.org   (253) 272-3500
Hours: Thurs - Sun, 10am - 5pm.
On the 3rd Thursday of each month, the History Museum is open until 8pm, with FREE admission from 2 - 8pm

History comes to life at this museum, which features interactive exhibits, theatrical storytelling, artifacts and more.

Admission: Not Provided

Westport Maritime Museum
2201 Westhaven Dr Westport, WA
www.westportmaritimemusem.com
(360) 268-0078

April - Sept: 10am - 4pm (Closed Tues & Wed); Oct Mar: 12pm - 4pm (Closed Tues., Wed., Christmas)

Paid Admission

White Pass Country Museum
12990 US Hwy 12 Packwood, WA
www.whitepasscountrymuseum.org
Hours: Winter Hours: Sat: Noon - 4pm;
Summer Hours: Thur, Fri & Sat: Noon - 5pm

Paid Admission

Wild Waves Theme Park
36201 Enchanted Prkwy S Federal Way, WA
www.wildwaves.com   (253) 661-8001
Hours: See online calendar - hours vary.

Water park that includes rides and games for kids and kids at heart! Also features special events.
Admission: Not Provided

Metho River Raft & Kayak
27 Rader Rd Winthrop, WA
www.methowrafting.com/   (509) 341-4661

Whitewter rafting, kayaking, scenic tours and river
tubing.

Admission: Not Provided

Wolf Haven International
3111 Offut Lake Rd Tenino, WA
www.wolfhaven.org   (800) 448-9653
- Spring/Summer Hours:
  Mon/Wed-Sat: 10am-4pm; Sun: Noon - 4pm.
  Closed every Tuesday.
- Fall/Winter Hours: Weekends only.
  Sat: 10am - 4pm; Sun: Noon - 4.
  Closed to the public February 16 - March 16.

Paid Attraction

Wonderland Family Fun Center
10515 N Division Spokane, WA
www.wonderlandusa.com   (509) 488-4386
- Fall Hours: Sun - 11am to 9pm;
  Mon-Thurs: 2pm to 9pm; Fri: 2pm-11pm;
  Sat: 10am-11pm.
- Consult site for winter, spring and summer hours

Paid Attraction

Woodland Park Zoo
5500 Phinney Ave N Seattle, WA
www.zoo.org   (206) 548-2500
Hours: Daily, Except Christmas Day.
        Oct 1, 2015 - Apr 30, 2016: 9:30am - 4pm;
        May 1, 2016 - Sept 2016: 9:30am - 6pm

Paid Attraction

World Kite Museum
303 Sid Snyder Dr Long Beach, WA
www.kitefestival.com   (360) 642-4020
- October - March: Fri - Tues, 11am - 5pm;
- Apr - Sept: daily, 11am - 5pm

Paid Attraction

Yakima Area Arboretum
1401 Arboretum Dr Yakima, WA
www.ahtrees.org   (509) 248-7337
Hours: Daily, dawn - dusk

Admission: Not Provided

Yakima Valley Museum
2105 Tieton Dr Yakima, WA
www.yakimavalleymuseum.org/   (509) 248-0747

Admission: Not Provided

Yakima Valley Rail & Steam Museum
10 Asotin Ave Toppenish, WA
www.nprymuseum.org/   (509) 865-1191

Admission: Not Provided

Zip San Juan
1st St in the turn around by Court House
Friday Harbor, WA
www.zipsanjuan.com   (360) 378-5947

Paid Attraction

Alphabetical Events & Attractions List

Aberdeen
17th Annual Aberdeen Art Walk & Rod Fest
Splash 2015 Annual Waterfront Festival
The Aberdeen Museum of History

Algona
Algona Days

Anacortes
Anacortes Arts Festival
Anacortes Kayak Tours
Island Adventures Whale Watching
Skagit River Salmon Festival

Arlington
Absolute Air Park
Arlington Fly in WWII Bomber
Red Rooster Route Family Farm Fun
Stillaguamish Festival of the River & Pow Wow
The Outback Kangaroo Farm

Auburn
3rd Annual Car Show 4 Kids
Auburn 4th of July Festival
Auburn Good Ol' Days
Auburn Winter Bus Barn Bonanza
Auburn's Petpalooza 2016
Bus Barn Bonanza
Halloween Harvest Festival
The Little Farm at Windwater

Bainbridge Island
Bainbridge Island Summer Studio
Grand Old Fourth of July Celebration & Street Fair

Bellevue

Bellevue Arts Museum ARTSfair
Bellevue Family 4th of July
Bellevue Festival of the Arts
Bellevue Hilltop Holiday Craft Show
Bellevue Live at Lunch
Bellevue Strawberry Festival
Bellevue Wedding Expo
Cultural Crossroads Festival
Garden d'Lights
KidsQuest Children's Museum
Snowflake Lane
Vasa Park Christmas Craft Show

Bellingham

Bellingham Farmers Market - Downtown
Bellingham Sportsplex
Jump Around Fun Zone
Mt. Baker Rhythm & Blues Festival

Birch Bay

Birch Bay Waterslides

Blaine

An Old Fashioned Fourth of July
Art 2 Jazz Street Fair
Birch Bay Waterslides
Drayton Harbor Days Festival
Miniature World Family Fun Center

Bothell

2015 My Friends & More Holiday Bazaar
Bothell Farmers Market
Bothell Farmers Market Kids Day
Elevated Sportz Ultimate Trampoline Park
& Event Center
Holiday Harvest Craft Show

Pirate Day

Safe Halloween

St. Brendan School Holiday Craft Fair

The Country Village

Witches Night Out

Wizard Fest

Woodinville Holiday Craft Fair

Bremerton

Bremerton Blackberry Festival

Bremerton Children's Bug & Reptile Museum

Bremerton Summer Brewfest

Kitsap County Fair & Stampede

Play Indoor Playground & Learning Center

Brush Prairie

Hockinson Holiday Bazaar

Burien

Kennedy Arts & Crafts Faire

Shorewood Holiday Bazaar

Burlington

26th Annual A Note-able Affair Craft Fair

Children's Museum of Skagit County

Camas

Camas Days

Camas Farmers Market

Silver Bells 4th Christmas Bazaar

Carnation

A Festival for May

Harvest Festival

Midsummer Festival

Remlinger Farms Tours

Chehalis
Chehalis Garlic Fest & Craft Show

Lewis County Historical Museum

Veterans Memorial Museum

Chelan
Echo Valley Ski Area

Lake Chelan Fine Arts Festival

Slide Waters Lake Chelan Slidepark

Cheney
Cheney Historical Museum

Chewelah
Chewelah Chataqua

Chimacum
Chimacum Arts & Crafts Fair

Colville
Northeast Washington Fair

Conconully
Conconully Outdoor Quilt & Craft Show

Cowboy Caviar Fete

Conconully
Outdoor Quilt and Craft Show

Coulee Dam
4th of July Festival of America

Coupeville
Coupeville Arts & Crafts Festival

Coupeville Farmers Market

Penn Cove Mussel Festival

Covington
Covington Days Festival

Crystal Mountain
Crystal Mountain Ski Resort

Dallesport

FLY-IN (Dallesport/Murdock fire department fundraiser)

Darrington

Summer Meltdown Festival

Davenport

Davenport Pioneer Days

DuPont

DuPont Historical Museum

Easton

Hyak Sno-Park Sledding Hill

Eastsound

Orcas Island Historical Museum

Outer Island Excursions

The Funhouse Commons

Eatonville

Northwest Trek Wildlife Park

Pioneer Farm Museum & Ohop Indian Village

Edmonds

A Taste of Edmonds

Edmonds Art Festival 2016

Edmonds Historical Museum

Edmonds July 4th Celebration

Edmonds Woodway High School Music Boosters Craft Fair

Elbe

Mt. Ranier Scenic Railroad

Ellensburg

Kittlas County Fair

Enumclaw

Enumclaw Rotary Street Fair

King County Fair

Everett

Children's Music in the Park Series
Cinema Under the Stars
Colors of Freedom 4th of July Festival
Everett Craft Beer Festival
Everett Fall Home Show
Everett Fall Wedding Expo
Everett Gift Show
Everett Sausage Festival
Festival of Artists
Flying Heritage Collection
Future of Flight Aviation Center & Boeing Tour
Imagine Children's Museum
Music in the Park at the Marina
Music in the Park Waterfront Series
Sorticulture Garden Art Festival
Street Tunes
Washington State Everett Fall Home Show
Wintertide Celebration

Federal Way

Wild Waves Theme Park

Ferndale

Art in the Park

Fort Lewis

Celebrate Independence Day FreedomFest

Friday Harbor

A Place to Play for Kids
San Juan County Fair
San Juan Historical Museum
San Juan Island Summer Arts Fair
San Juan Island Whale & Wildlife Tours
San Juan Safaris Whale Watch & Wildlife
The Whale Museum

Friday Harbor
Zip San Juan

Gig Harbor
Gig Harbor Summer Art Festival

Harbor History Museum

TideFest Fine Arts & Crafts Celebration

Winterfest Arts & Crafts Fair

Gold Bar
2015 Gold Dust Days

Graham
Pierce County Fair

Granger
Cherry Hill Family Golf Course

Grapeview
Mason/Benson Craft Bazaar

Grayland
Beachcombers Driftwood Show

Cranberry Harvest Festival

Windrider's Kite Festival

Grays Harbor
Gray's Harbor County Fair

Home Valley
Bigfoot Bash & Bounty

Hoquaim
21st Annual Grays Harbor Shore Bird Festival

Hoquiam
Polson History Museum

Ilwaco
Ilwaco Saturday Market

Ilwaco Summer Saturday Market

Index
12th Annual Index Arts Festival

Issaquah

- Bicycle Adventures
- Christmas in Telemark
- Cougar Mountain Zoo
- Cougar Mountain Zoo
- Evergreen Mountain Bike Festival 2016
- Fenders on Front Street
- Issaquah Fall Farmers Market
- Issaquah Reindeer Festival
- Issaquah Salmon Hatchery
- Pickering Barn Christmas Craft Show
- Saturday Summer Farmers Market

Kelso

- Kelso Highlander Festival and Scottish Games

Kennewick

- Creation Festival 2015
- Lighted Boat Parade
- Mid-Columbia Duck Race
- Southridge Music Booster's Holiday Bazaar

Kent

- Kent Commons Holiday Bazaar
- Kent Cornucopia Days
- Kent Holiday Craft Market
- Kent International Festival 2016
- Kent Kids' Art Day 2016
- Kent Valley Ice Centre

Kingston

- Kitsap Arts & Crafts Festival

Kirkland

- Kirkland Summerfest

Lacey

- Charlie's Safari
- Festive Shopping Experience Bazaar

Homemade for the Holidays
Lacey Holiday Bazaar
Pacific Northwest Mushroom Festival
Thurston County Fair

Lake Chelan

Lake Chelan Evening Farmers Market
Winterfest

Lake Stevens

Lake Stevens Aquafest

Lakewood

Lakewood Summerfest

Langley

Choochokam Arts & Music Festival
Island County Fair

Leavenworth

Dirty Face Music Fest
Icicle Village Resort
Leavenworth Lions Craft Fair
Leavenworth Oktoberfest
Washington State Autumn Leaf Festival

Lemt

Carpinito Brothers' Pumpkin Patch, Corn Maze &
Farm Fun Yard

Long Beach

Columbia-Pacific Market
Funland
Holidays at the Beach
Sandsations Sand Castle Competition
World Kite Museum

Longmire

Longmire Mineral Hot springs
Longmire Museum

Longview

Cowlitz County Fair & Rodeo

Lyle

Northwest Homesteading Fair

Lynden

Lynden Raspberry Festival

Northwest Washington Fair

Raspberry Festival

Lynnwood

Lynnwood Ice Center

The Rootbeer Store Tastings

Marysville

Marysville Strawberry Festival 2016

Marysville Street Festival

McCleary

McCleary Bear Festival

Mead

Cat Tales

Cat Tales Zoological Park

Cherry Picker's Trot

Mt. Spokane Skiing

Medical Lake

Blue Waters Bluegrass Festival

Mercer Island

Mercer Island Summer Celebration

Mill Creek

Mill Creek Festival

Monroe

Evergreen State Fair

Homespun Spring Bazaar 2016

Hot Rod Gallery Museum

Kangaroo Cottage

NWESC's 5th Annual Holiday Bazaar

Monroe

Oktoberfest Monroe

Washington State Evergreen Fall RV Show

Morton

Morton Historic Railroad Depot

Moses Lake

Grant County Fair

Surf 'n Slide Water Park

Mount Vernon

Skagit County Fair

Mountlake Terrace

Mountlake Terrace High Holiday Bazaar

Mukilteo

Mukilteo Lighthouse Festival

Traxx Indoor Racing

Neah Bay

Makah Cultural & Research Center

Newport

Newport Music Festival

Pend Oreille Valley Lavender Festival

North Bend

Festival at Mount Si

North Vancouver (CANADA)

North Vancouver Holiday Bazaar

Oak Harbor

Oak Harbor Music Festival

Oak Harbor's Old-Fashioned 4th OH July

Ocean Shores

Find Yer' Treasure Gift Fair

Ocean Shores Arts & Crafts Festival

Ocean Shores Beach Blast

Winter Fanta-Sea Craft Show

Ocosta

Children's Hospital Craft Show

Odessa

Deutschesfest Street Fair

Okanogan

Loup Loup Skiing

Okanogan County Fair

Olalla

Olalla Bluegrass & Beyond Festival

Olga

Orcas Island Trail Rides

Olympia

Capital Lake Fair

Hands On Children's Museum

Home Made for the Holidays Bazaar

Littlerock Elementary's 67th Annual Winterfest

Nisqually National Wildlife Refuge

Olympia High School Bearzaar

Olympic Flight Museum

The Farmers Market of Olympia

The State Capital Museum

Onasket

Family-A-Fair

Orting

Orting Bike Trail

Orting Pumpkin Fest

Otis Orchards

The Pottery Bug

Packwood

    Packwood Fall Craft Fair

    Packwood Mountain Festival

    White Pass Country Museum

Pasco

    Pasco Christmas Arts & Crafts Show

Port Angeles

    Clallam County Fair

    Dream Playground

    Dungeness Crab & Seafood Festival

    Hoh Rain Forest

    Marymere Falls Trail

    Moments in Time Trail

    Sol Duc Falls Trail

Port Gamble

    Old Mill Days

    Port Gamble Country Christmas

Port Orchard

    Festival by the Bay

    Port Orchard Chocolate Festival

    Port Orchard Summer Artwalk

    Port Orchard Art Walk

    Sidney Museum & Arts

Port Townsend

    Crafts by the Dock

    Holiday Craft Sale 2015

    Jefferson County Fair

    Uptown Crafts Fair

    Wooden Boat Festival

Poulsbo

    North Kitsap Holiday Fest

Pullman

Autumn Arts & Crafts Festival

National Lentil Festival

Pullman's 40th Annual 4th of July Celebration

Puyallup

A Victorian Country Christmas Festival

Celebration of Western & Wildlife Art Show

Funky Junk Sisters: Junk Salvation

Great Train Expo

Meeker Days Festival

Meeker Mansion Craft Show

Northwest Woodcarvers Show & Sale

NWCA 35th Annual "Artistry in Wood" Show & Sale

Oktoberfest Northwest

Puyallup Gem Faire

Puyallup Girls Night Out

The Daffodil Festival

Tiffany's Skate Roller Skating & Family Fun Center

Washington Sportsmen's Show

Washington Spring Fair

Washington State Health, Fitness & Beauty Expo

Raymond

Northwest Carriage Museum

Redmond

75th Annual Derby Days

K1 Speed Seattle

Mobile Food Rodeo 2015

Redmond Derby Days

Renton

Hassle Free Holiday Bazaar

HUGE PRE-BLACK FRIDAY HOLIDAY BAZAAR

Renton Fall Harvest Festival

Renton River Days

Richland

Badger Mountain School Holiday Bazaar

Country Nesters Antiques in the Park Show

Market at the Parkway

Richland Art in the Park

Ridgefield

16th Annual Birdfest & Bluegrass Celebration

Clark County Fair

Ridgefield Fourth of July Festival

Washington State Horse Expo

Ritzville

The Railroad-Depot History Museum

Roy

Roy Fall Pioneer Rodeo

San Juan Island

San Juan Island Farmers Market

Seafood

SeafoodFest

SeaTac

Seattle Christian School Christmas Bazaar

TYEE Holiday Bazaar

Seattle

2015 Northwest Fall Art & Fine Craft Show

2015 Seattle Craft Fair

2015 Seattle International Gem & Jewelry Show

2nd Annual Seattle Children's Festival

Alki Art Fair

Argosy Cruises & Tillicum Village

BabyFest

Bill Speidel's Underground Tour

Burke Museum

Burke Museum of Natural History & Culture

Seattle

- DragonFest & Night Market
- EMP Museum
- Fine Art & Holiday Gifts at Fauntleroy
- Fremont First Friday Art Walk
- Fremont Street Summer Solstice Fair
- Fremont Summer First Friday Art walk
- FrenchFest
- Georgetown Carnival
- Georgetown Morgue
- Great Wallingford Wurst Festival
- Groupon Bite of Seattle
- International Children's Festival 2016
- Japanese Tea Gardens
- Lake Union Wooden Boat Festival
- Magnolia Summerfest
- Martin Luther King Jr Birthday Celebration & March
- Morgan Junction Community Festival 2016
- Museum of Flight
- Museum of History & Industry
- Night Market & Moon Festival
- Northwest African American Museum
- Northwest Folklife Festival
- Pacific Science Center
- Pike Place Market
- Ride the Ducks
- SalmonFest Seattle
- School of Acrobatics & New Circus Arts
- Seafair Milk Carton Derby
- Seafair Summer Fourth
- Seattle Aquarium
- Seattle Art Museum

Seattle

- Seattle Center
- Seattle Chinese Garden
- Seattle Holiday Craft Fair
- Seattle Mini-Maker Faire
- Seattle Pet Expo
- Seattle Reptile Expo
- Seattle Street Food Festival
- Seattle Waterfront Harbor Sightseeing Tour Cruise
- Seattle Women's Life Style Expo
- Wedgwood Art Festival
- West Seattle Summer Fest
- Woodland Park Zoo

Sedro Woolley

- North Cascades National Park

Selah

- Selah 4th of July Celebration

Sequim

- 2015 Holiday Bazaar
- Dungeness Spit National Wildlife Refuge
- Olympic Game Farm
- Olympic Peninsula Adventures
- Sequim Irrigation Festival & Street Fair
- Sequim Lavender Fiesta

Shoreline

- NW SolarFest Sustainable Living Fair

Silvana

- Silvana Fair

Silverlake

- 7 Wonders Museum

Snohomish

- Blackman House Museum
- Craven Farm's Fall Festival & Corn Maze

Snohomish

Echo Falls Holiday Home & Gift Show
Ground Frog Day
Kla Ha Ya Days
Snohomish Farmers Market
Snohomish Pumpkin Hurl & Medieval Faire
Nightmare on I-9

Snoqualmie

Friendship With Thomas
Snoqualmie Railroad Days

Spokane

14th Great Northwest Nationals
1909 Looff Carrousel
Children's Museum of Spokane
Fall Folk Festival 2015
Inland Northwest Craft Beer Festival
Pavilion Amusement Rides
Pig Out in the Park
Science Center of Spokane
Sky Ride Over the Falls
Splash Down
Spokane Christmas Arts & Crafts Show
Spokane Community College Art/Craft/Food Fair
Spokane Renaissance Faire
Wonderland Family Fun Center

Spokane Valley

2015 ValleyFest
Splash Down Family Waterpark
Spokane County Interstate Fair
University High School Fall Craft Fair
Valleyfest

Stanwood

Art By The Bay

Stanwood Camano Community Fair

Stevenson

Columbia Gorge Bluegrass Festival

Skamania County Fair & Timber Carnival

Sultan

Sultan Summer Shindig Festival

Sumner

Rhubarb Days

Tacoma

27th Annual Ethnic Fest Celebration

African-American Museum of Washington

Children's Museum of Tacoma

Deep Forest Challenge

Ethnic Fest 2015

Job Carr Cabin Museum

Ladies Auxiliary Fall Bazaar

Music & Art in Wright Park

Point Defiance Zoo & Aquarium

Proctor Arts Fest

Slater Museum of Natural History

Tacoma Fall Wedding Expo

Tacoma Freedom Fair

Tacoma Holiday Food & Gift Festival

Tacoma Home & Garden Show

Tacoma Wedding Expo

Taste of Tacoma

Washington State History Museum

Tacoma

South Sound Craft Beer Festival

Tenino

Wolf Haven International

Tieton

Highland Community Days

Toledo

31st Annual Mt. St. Helens Bluegrass Festival

Mount St. Helens Bluegrass Festival

Toppenish

Northern Pacific Railway Museum

Yakima Valley Rail & Steam Museum

Tukwila

Backyard Wildlife Festival

Sykart Indoor Racing Center (Washington)

Tulalip

Hibulb Cultural Center & Natural History Preserve

University Place

University Place Sun Fest

University Place Winter Fest

Vancouver

10th Annual Children's Festival

2nd Annual North Vancouver Holiday Bazaar

Archaeology Kids Digs!

Bell Ringer Bazaar

Clark County Historical Museum

Crystal Plum Bazaar

Dizzy Castle

Ft. Vancouver National Park

JJ Jump

Mountain View High School Holiday Bazaar

Old Apple Tree Festival

Recycled Arts Festival 2016

Vashon

Vashon Farmers Market

Vashon Island Strawberry Festival

Walla Walla

Arcade-ia

Downtown Farmers Market

Fort Walla Walla Museum

Jumpin' Jelly Beanz

Jumpin' Jelly Beanz!

Kirkman House Museum

Walla Walla Fair & Frontier Days

Washougal

Washougal High School Holiday Marketplace

Wenatchee

Washington Apple Blossom Fair 2016

Wenatchee Fall Arts & Crafts Show

Westport

69th Annual Seafood Festival & Craft Show

Annual Fleur de Lis Festival

Booming Bay Fireworks

Crush Me, Squeeze Me, Make Me Wine at the Beach Festival

Lighthouse Haunted Halloween

Maritime Museum's Ole Fashioned 4th

Rusty Scupper's Pirate Daze

Santa by the Sea

Westport Art Festival

Westport Blues Festival

Westport Maritime Museum

Westport Seafood Festival

World Class Crab Races & Feed

White Salmon

I'm Dreaming of a White Salmon Holiday Festival

Wickersham

Lake Whatcom Railway

Winthrop

Methow River Raft & Kayak

Woodinville

Celebrate Woodinville

Woodinville Women's Show

Yakima

Central Washington State Fair

McAllister Museum of Aviation

Meadowbrook Family Fun Center

Yakima Area Arboretum

Yakima Folklife Festival

Yakima Valley Museum